Vintage WRISTWATCHES

Reyne Haines

Published by

krause publications
A subsidiary of F+W Media, Inc.

700 East State Street • Iola, WI 54990-0001
715-445-2214 • 888-457-2873
www.krausebooks.com

To order books or other products call toll-free 1-800-258-0929 or visit us online at www.krausebooks.com or www.Shop.Collect.com.

Cover photography by Kris Kandler
Omega, *Speedmaster, automatic, stainless steel, circa 1980s.* $1,200
Watch courtesy of Chris Miller

Library of Congress Control Number: 2009937510

ISBN-13: 978-1-4402-0409-8
ISBN-10: 1-4402-0409-8

Designed by Rachael Knier
Edited by Mark Moran

Printed in China

Foreword by Al Bandiero |5|

A Special Thanks |6|

———————

For Those with Time on Their Hands… |8|
  Identifying and Evaluating Wristwatches |10|
  What's It Worth? |10|
    The Wristwatch Run-Through |11|

Watches Listed Alphabetically by Maker |13|

———————

Watch Terminology |248|

Resources |250|

  Clubs and Associations |250|
  Web Sites and Online Groups |251|

About the Author |252|

Index |253|

Breitling "Navitimer", for details please see page 28.

Watch courtesy of Derek Dier,
WatchesToBuy.com

FOREWORD BY AL BANDIERO

*W*atches. Why do I like them? The answer is simple, and yet not so simple. I once received a wonderful piece of advice: "You can tell a man by his shoes and his watch." From the moment I heard this, it never left my mind and set a rule that I've tried to live by. My only problem was, at the time I could not afford to buy the kind of watches I liked.

When my career started to build, the first item I bought was a Rolex watch — blue face, silver clip band. It was beautiful. I remember walking into the store to buy it, putting it on my wrist and looking at it every minute for hours. It seemed the hands never moved because I looked at it so often. From one watch, my collection grew to 40: Breitling, Franchi, Minotti, to name a few. And, one that means a lot to me: a tri-colored gold pocket watch that was given to my father as a Confirmation gift when he was 13 years old.

Make no mistake about it: People notice the watch a person is wearing within the first minute they meet. When I became a series regular on TV, I wore a watch in the first scene I was in, with my arms crossed. I cannot tell you how many people later told me they liked the watch, and wanted to know what brand it was.

To me, watches are like people: Each has a different personality, and will tell people your personality before they get to know you. Whether you own one or 40, it doesn't matter, because there is no other item one can wear (outside of a wedding band) that is more personal.

I love fashion, yet fashions will always go in and out of style. A watch that means something to you is timeless. It is not something you just go out and buy. You study it. You say to yourself, "Is this me?" When someone else buys you a watch, you can tell if they truly know the kind of person you are. My wife knows exactly who I am, and each watch she buys me fits me perfectly. We live by time every day of our lives — "Am I on time ... running late … am I early?" Knowing that, wear a watch that makes you feel good every time you look at it.

I will close by passing along something my mother told me when I was a kid. She said, "Always buy quality. If you can't afford it at the time, save until you can." She also said to me, "People who know quality can always tell quality … and for the people who don't, it doesn't matter."

If you haven't noticed the watch someone is wearing, maybe now you will.

Born and raised in Brooklyn, N.Y., Bandiero was an on-air personality in New York City for many years. He started his acting career by appearing in the film *Rocky IV*. Since then, he has worked extensively in film and television. He lives in Los Angeles.

A SPECIAL THANKS

When the opportunity to write Vintage Wristwatches came my way, I jumped at the chance. Watches were one of my first collecting passions.

From the beginning, we've had clear goals for how we wanted the book to look: the quality of the photography, and background on all of the manufacturers. I spent many years as the moderator for the watch discussion group for TIAS (The Internet Antique Shop, www.tias.com) and greatly enjoyed the interaction between its members, discussing new and old watches alike.

As an appraiser, dealer and collector, I've specialized in 20th-century decorative arts, and am called upon to appraise collectibles ranging from antique watches to $20 million paintings.

I've been lucky enough to regularly appear as an expert in the media, including as a recurring special guest on The Early Show on CBS and in numerous publications including The Wall Street Journal, The Washington Post, The Chicago Tribune, The Los Angeles Times, Home & Garden, Hemisphere Magazine, Worth Magazine, TV Guide, Family Circle Magazine, Time Out New York, Traditional Home, Romantic Home, Inspire Magazine and Collectors Weekly. I am also a blogger for The Huffington Post and may be heard on Martha Stewart Living Radio on the Sirius Satellite Radio Network.

In 2003, I wrote The Art of Glass for the Dayton, Ohio, Art Institute. I've contributed to books including Antiques Roadshow Collectibles by Carol Prisant and Adventures at the Auction by Leslie Hindman. I also penned the introduction to the 2009 Warman's Companion — Watches, and a chapter on investing

in Tiffany for the 2010 edition of Warman's Antiques and Collectibles Price Guide.

My professional background has included working as a model, news announcer and journalist. I keep busy as the owner of The Finer Things in New York City, a company that acquires and sells luxury goods for clients at auction and privately. I've also created "Three or More ... A Perspective on Antiques, Collecting and Pop Culture," found at www.threeormore.net.

In addition to my editor, Mark F. Moran, I'd like to thank several auction houses that so graciously offered to loan images and information on watches they have sold over the last year: Leslie Hindman Auctioneers in Chicago, Heritage Auction Galleries in Dallas, Bonham's in Los Anegeles, and Antiquorum.

Coming up with 1,200 images for this book was quite the task. It doesn't seem like a large number until you start cataloging them. Then it seems daunting.

I think one of the reasons anyone gets into collecting is because of the camaraderie you experience amongst other collectors. When I reached out to friends that I knew had watch collections, they were quick to offer up their treasures for me to show the world. Jim Dicke, collector of new and old alike, you have amazing taste. You were one of the first people I reached out to in hopes of photographing your collection. Thanks so much for saying yes! Chris Miller, I had no idea your collecting passion extended past art glass. Thank you so much for pulling your beauties out of the safe and for being so generous with the time I could use them. Phil Lucas, I always thought of you as the man with the best collection of bumper-wind Omegas. Little did I know your watch passion extended to so many other brands. Derek Dier, your passion for collecting can be seen in each e-mail you sent, and the powerful images you were able to offer. I appreciate all the time you took putting together the variety of watches for this book, and when I needed more than our original count, you were quick to come to my aid. Charlie Cleves, everyone should know you. I have never met a more dedicated, knowledgeable, passionate watch collector/dealer in my life. Anyone reading this book that doesn't know you should certainly make it a point to introduce themselves.

Tim Haines, I appreciate the love of collecting wristwatches we shared over the years. I believe it was one of the first things we found we had in common. No doubt, I will remember the stories of your many wristwatch-buying adventures for years to come.

For everyone else who gave me advice, offered suggestions when I was having writers block, or was just interested in knowing more about the project — I thank you for your support (and look for me to call you with my next project!)

FOR THOSE WITH
TIME ON THEIR HANDS...

*B*eing a collector of many things, I have always found the wristwatch to be a fun "collectible." Not only is there an interesting back-story behind the company that made it, it also has function.

They take up little space, so you can collect in volume, and there is a price range to suite anyone's budget.

Many people collect things because they find them aesthetically pleasing. Certainly, most watches could be perceived as tiny works of art. They are found in a dizzying array of shapes, dial designs, and colors. Some have even been made in conjunction with artists (i.e. Andy Warhol) while others were designed with a specific painting in mind (Salvador Dali's "Persistence of Memory.)

Some watch companies designed their products for the masses, others for the classes.

Some collectors want only certain brands, while others look to acquire one of everything. There are collectors that only want things in pink gold. Others just buy chronographs. Then there are others who love them all!

Watch designs have changed greatly over the last 100+ years. The first company to manufacture a wristwatch was Patek Philippe. It was designed in 1868 and sold to the Countess Koscowicz of Hungary in 1876. It was wound with a key, and had gold panels on each side of the dial encrusted with diamonds.

Before World War I, wristwatches were thought of as jewelry, and meant for women only. During the war, soldiers needed to have access to their watches quickly, and were often unable to reach into their pockets to check the time. Their watches were worn on their wrists for easy access. They were called "trench watches" and were made out of pocket-watch movements that were big and bulky. Often the winding crown was at the 12 o'clock position. From that point on, they were no longer seen as just for ladies.

In 1923, the first self-winding movement was produced by Swiss watchmaker John Harwood. This type of movement would wind using the motion of the wearer's arm. An internal weight would rotate back and forth as the watch moved, keeping the watch wound for approximately 12 hours.

The next evolution of the watch would be the creation of the electronic movement, which never needed winding. It was designed by the Hamilton Watch Co. in 1957 and was called the "Hamilton Electric." It was an instant hit with consumers. Unfortunately, technology was soon to change and Hamilton ceased production of the line in 1969.

In the 1960s, several Swiss firms began designing quartz watch movements. The Swiss decided not to pursue production of quartz movements, as the cost to overhaul their factories was prohibitive, and it would put many watchmakers out of work.

The Japanese, however, moved ahead with the quartz designs. In 1969, Seiko would place their first quartz wristwatch on the market. This type movement was more accurate than a mechanical watch, and quickly gained a large portion of the marketplace. Not only was it more accurate than a mechanical watch, it never needed winding. And a quartz movement would not need regular servicing like a mechanical watch. It merely needed a battery replacement over time. Numerous Swiss and American watch manufacturers withered before Japanese dominance. Many closed their doors, or filed bankruptcy.

Whether you are a novice or seasoned collector, this book was designed with everyone in mind. It's part eye candy, and part educational.

It opens with information on identification. There were a great number of watch manufacturers around the world producing fine timepieces over the last 100+ years. Some watch companies designed the complete watch, while others designed the case and dial, and partnered with another company to provide them with their movements. We've even seen some watch manufacturers produce watches under different brand names.

We also discuss the never-ending question of "What's it worth?" There is never a simple answer. There are a number of factors that go into determining the value of wristwatches. What is the condition? What is the case material? Is the case sterling, stainless steel, gold or platinum? Who made the movement?

The majority of the book takes a look at the history of American and European wristwatch manufacturers from A-Z. We discuss when they were founded, where and by whom. Also, we feature some of the highs (and a few lows) they experienced over their years in business.

Along with the individual company information we offer an array of images of different timepieces each company made. Keep in mind this is not a catalog of each line made. With each photo is a brief description of the watch illustrated, and what it has recently sold for, either at auction or privately. Remember, as I mentioned before, there are many factors that play into the value of each watch represented.

Interspersed throughout this book are original advertisements for watches found in newspapers and magazines starting around the early 1910s. I have always enjoyed looking at ads because they tell us so much we might not have already known. For example, the cost of the watch originally, the name of the line, when it was made, and what options were offered.

For the new watch collector, learning a little watch terminology can go a long way. We answer the question: What is a tourbillion? What does chronometer mean? What are jewels? What is a pusher used for? This section offers a broad array of commonly used, and not so commonly used, watch "words" to help clear up any confusion.

Finally, one of the great aspects of collecting is meeting others with similar collecting interests. Joining a local collectors club, or even one online, can greatly expand your collecting horizons. There are links to Web sites filled with information on collecting, where to find parts or local a watchmaker for a repair, message boards to learn more about new acquisitions, and more!

Identifying and Evaluating Wristwatches

There are a few key factors that play a role in identifying and evaluating wristwatches. These seemingly small factors can make a large difference in value and desirability among collectors.

Who Made It?

Obviously, one of the first things you want to know is, "Who made my watch?" Many times the answer is simple. Who's name is on the dial? However, there are other instances that may make that answer not as obvious as you might think.

There are some timepieces that do not have a name on the dial. Others that just say, "Swiss." You may have to open the back to determine who made the movement to help identify the maker. The manufacturer of the movement does not always mean that is who made the watch. Check the inside of the case to see if there are any other markings that might reveal the maker's name.

Though you may find a name on the dial, there may be a different name on the movement. Occasionally, watchmakers would contract with movement manufacturers. For example, you will often find this to be the case with watches marked "Tiffany & Co." on the dial.

Finally, there are certain brands that used more than one name for different lines. For example, Rolex watches are most commonly branded "Rolex" on the dial, however, they also made lines of watches marked Tudor, Unicorn, Marconi, Rolco and Genex.

What's It Worth?

Value is also something that is not always black and white. There are numerous factors that play into evaluating a wristwatch. Some of them are:

1. Condition: As with just about another other collectible, condition plays a huge role in value. A mint-condition watch can be worth $500, and the same watch in good condition can be worth $100. How clean is the dial? Is the luminescence on the hands and bar markers crisp? Does the watch have its original box and papers? Is the band and clasp original, or replacement? Finally, does it run? If so, is it keeping accurate time? These are all factors that seasoned dealers and collectors consider when pricing a watch.

2. Availability: Is this a watch that was made for the masses or made in limited production? Is this a watch made to commemorate a certain event?

3. Lineage: You won't often hear mention of a watch's provenance, but if your watch was previously owned by a celebrity, the value can certainly increase.

4. Monograms: Much like buying a monogrammed piece of silver, unless it is your initials, collectors often don't want someone else's name, business affiliation, wedding anniversary, etc. on their watch.

5. Box and papers: Collectors love acquiring wristwatches that come with their original box and paperwork. Not only is it fun to have, it can increase the value of the watch. (Don't despair if they don't have these items.)

6. Case materials: Often, a line of watches might have been produced in more than one type of metal. The value of a wristwatch can greatly change from one material to another.

With all of the above said, when selling a watch, you have to consider additional things such as:

1. Where to sell it: Will you sell your watch to a dealer, via the Internet, at a watch show, or at a publicized auction? If you have a more common watch, I'd suggest selling it on one of the many watch-collecting Web sites. There are always collectors looking at the classifieds. If your watch is something harder to find, or a bit more desirable, it might be best if you reach out to one of the jewelry and watch auction houses to help gain the most interest in your piece.

2. When to sell it: Not only does where you sell it make a difference, but so does when you sell it. There are "seasons" for selling things. Collectors can be fickle. The market is ever changing. What is hot today can quickly become yesterday's news. Collectors vying for that certain series in a brand, with that certain colored dial, vintage, etc., can move on to the next hot thing in collecting in no time.

On a final note, the prices illustrated in this book are merely a guide. Most are actual prices realized at auction. Things are worth whatever someone is willing to pay on any given day. Some areas of the world are able to get more for certain watches than others. Again, the desirability of any given watch fluctuates.

THE WRISTWATCH RUN-THROUGH

Not so long ago, if you wanted to learn more about wristwatches, you had to find a watchmaker, join the local chapter of the National Association of Watch and Clock Collectors, read a book, or wait for a watch show to come to your area.

Today, collecting and learning about collecting has become considerably easier. The Internet has paved the way for people to find unlimited amounts of information on wristwatch restoration, locating parts for a watch in need of repair (or a watchmaker, if you aren't mechanically inclined), meeting dealers and private enthusiasts who collect via message boards and online discussion groups, and the ability to view hundreds of thousands of watches for sale with a few clicks of the mouse.

The Internet has also changed the face of who is collecting. Thought to be an "older gentleman's" market for quite some time, young male and female collectors alike have been popping up around the world. Collecting wristwatches has never had such a broad appeal!

Many of the younger collectors tend to gravitate towards the more modern watches, just the same as their tastes are often in the modern arena for furniture and decorative arts. The appeal of any of the asymmetrical Hamilton Electrics, or the Accutrons, along with the bold statement a great Rolex Daytona or Submariner makes are often what you see this generation searching for.

We've seen a slight rise in the values of lady's watches because of the Internet over the past few years. lady's watches, however, seem to still be quite undervalued. Once thought of as "jewelry" only, many women have become fascinated with the history behind a watch, the inexpensive price to acquire stunning works of art encrusted with semi-precious and precious gemstones, and the uniqueness they bring to an outfit.

The Internet has helped collectors identify watches worn by their favorite celebrity, worn on the moon, in a car race, in their favorite action film, etc.

One of the not-so-positive aspects of Internet collecting is the sheer volume of reproductions out there posing as authentic watches. They turn up everywhere, with links to professionally designed Web sites offering the best of the best for a discount, or up for bid on an Internet auction. You must keep in mind the old saying, "If it looks to good to be true, it probably is."

Not everyone is trying to put one over on you, but there are a few other concerns that should be addressed. One person's definition of "excellent condition" may not be the same as yours. Some people are more accepting of "wear and age" than you might be.

So between dodging reproductions, and trying to determine if an authentic watch is in an acceptable condition for you to want to acquire it, there are a few questions you should consider asking anyone online before opening your wallet:

1. Many people assume if it doesn't say it's a reproduction, it's authentic. Not necessarily so. Ask for a guarantee that the watch is authentic.

2. How did they acquire the watch?

3. Do they have the original receipt for the watch? (If they do not, it doesn't mean the watch is a reproduction, but if they do have the original receipt or paperwork, it helps you to feel more confident buying it).

4. Is the watch working? Seems like another question where the answer would be obvious. If you ask the question, you have the answer in writing, Should it arrive not working, you can go back to the seller.

5. How long have they had the watch? Is it something they recently purchased, or did they inherit it? If they are a collector selling some of their collection, the longer they've had it might give you confidence in how accurate their description of the watch is. The longer one collects, the more trained their eye becomes and the more knowledgeable they (hopefully) become.

6. What are the markings on the watch? Some case markings or movement markings will help you determine if the watch is all original, if the movement has been replaced, or might even tell you more about the period in which the watch was made.

7. Have they ever had the watch serviced? If yes, what work was done to it and when.

8. Ask for close-up images of the watch. Close-ups of the back, the dial and perhaps the band are a good idea. It is common practice for scammers to take a photo from someone else's Web site and use it to sell a fake, or to take your money and send you nothing in return. If you ask for additional photos, and they do not actually have the watch, it will quickly become obvious when they cannot provide the images you ask for.

9. What is their return policy if the watch is not as described? You should never buy a watch where there is no return privilege.

10. If possible, pay with a credit card. If the watch does not show up, or if it is not as described, you have recourse. If using Paypal, or another online payment program, look into buying insurance.

A LANGE & SÖHNE

*F*ounded by Adolph Lange in 1845 in Glashutte, Germany, this firm created some of the most coveted watches for a century. In 1875, Lange passed away and left the business to his sons, Richard and Emil. The company's headquarters were bombed on the last day of WWII in 1945 and production ceased. The company began creating fine timepieces again in 1990, headed up by Walter Lange, the great grandson of Adolph.

(Right)
A. LANGE & SÖHNE
- 18K yellow gold, power reserve, contemporary (back view below). *$12,000*
  Photos courtesy of James F. Dicke II

(Below)
A. LANGE & SÖHNE
- Glashutte, military oversize, rare. *$7,000*
  Watch courtesy of Charlie Cleves - Cleves and Lonnemann Jewelers

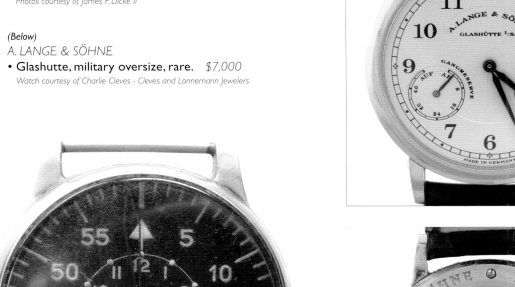

AUDEMARS PIGUET

Audemars Piguet was founded in 1875 in Le Brassus, Switzerland, by Jules-Louis Audemars and Edward-Auguste Piguet. In 1889 they exhibited a few of their more complicated watches at the Universal Exposition in Paris. Audemars Piguet is known for creating some of the "firsts" in watch movement history. In 1892 they created the first known minute repeater watch. In 1915, they created the smallest five-minute repeater movement. The first jump-hour watch was created in 1921. In 1946 came the world's smallest movement for a wristwatch at only 1.64mm thick.

Jules-Louis Audemars, left, and Edward-Auguste Piguet.

With the stock market crash in 1929 and then the Depression, most consumers were no longer able to purchase expensive watches. This forced Audemars Piguet (like many other Swiss watch companies) to lay off most of their workers. The company rebounded after 1932 with sales of their thin dress models and chronograph lines.

Audemars Piguet began experiencing stronger growth in the 1950s and '60s. The company partnered with Jaeger-LeCoultre in 1967 to create the world's thinnest automatic movement (2.55 mm)

Audemars signature watch, the Royal Oak, debuted in at the 1972 European watch-making fair in Basel. It was priced at 3,300 Swiss francs and was an instant hit. Audemars Piguet is still producing fine timepieces, all by hand.

(Right)
AUDEMARS PIGUET
• 18K yellow gold and diamonds, manual wind, 18K yellow gold bracelet. *$2,200*
Watch courtesy of Heritage Auction Galleries

(Far Right)
AUDEMARS PIGUET
• 18K yellow gold, modern. *$7,000*
Watch courtesy of Heritage Auction Galleries

(Above)
AUDEMARS PIGUET
- 18K yellow gold, manual wind, 14K yellow gold bracelet. *$1,500*

Watch courtesy of Heritage Auction Galleries

(Far Left)
AUDEMARS PIGUET
- 18K yellow gold. *$1,000*

Watch courtesy of Leslie Hindman Auctioneers

(Left)
AUDEMARS PIGUET,
- 18K yellow gold and lapis lazuli. *$1,500*

Watch courtesy of Leslie Hindman Auctioneers

(Below)
AUDEMARS PIGUET
- 18K yellow gold and diamonds. *$6,100*

Watch courtesy of Leslie Hindman Auctioneers

AUDEMARS PIGUET

• Genève, skeletonized, movement No. 174755, case No. B19713, 1960s. Self-winding, 18K yellow gold with an 18K yellow gold Audemars Piguet buckle. *$7,500*
Image courtesy of Antiquorum Auctioneers

AUDEMARS PIGUET

• Genève, movement No. 194787, case No. B 40430, late 1970s. Thin, 18K gold and an 18K gold Audemars Piguet buckle. *$1,500*
Image courtesy of Antiquorum Auctioneers

AUDEMARS PIGUET

• Genève, retailed by Gübelin, No. 93850, case No. 31861, early 1960s. Thin, platinum and diamond, with an integral textured 18K white gold mesh bracelet. *$5,000*
Image courtesy of Antiquorum Auctioneers

AUDEMARS PIGUET

• Genève, "Automatic," No. 61763, 1950s. Center seconds, self-winding, 18K yellow gold. *$3,000*
Image courtesy of Antiquorum Auctioneers

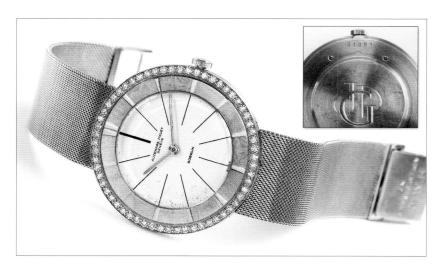

(Above)
AUDEMARS PIGUET
• Royal Oak, modern, stainless steel, 18K gold octagonal bezel secured with screws.   *$2,600*
  Watch courtesy of Heritage Auction Galleries

(Right)
AUDEMARS PIGUET
• Royal Oak, circa 2000, 18K yellow gold, No. D30664, model 2794, screw-down crown, quartz movement.   *$6,000*
  Watch courtesy of Heritage Auction Galleries

AUDEMARS PIGUET
- Lady's, circa 1975, 18K yellow gold, snap back, black bar markers, manual wind, 18K gold band. *$2,500*

Watch courtesy of Heritage Auction Galleries

AUDEMARS PIGUET
- Ultra thin, circa 1970s, gold bezel and sides, steel back, gold Dauphine hands, manual wind, two-tone bracelet, original inner and outer boxes and five extra links. *$1,200*

Watch courtesy of Heritage Auction Galleries

AUDEMARS PIGUET FOR TIFFANY & CO.
- Circa 1950s, 18K yellow gold, diamond-set case and band, gold bar markers, 18K with diamonds band, Tiffany box. *$2,000*

Watch courtesy of Heritage Auction Galleries

AUDEMARS PIGUET
- 18K yellow gold, curved Calatrava-style lugs, circa 1944. *$3,000*

Watch courtesy of Heritage Auction Galleries

AUDEMARS PIGUET
- 18K gold, baton numeral indicators, manual-wind, 18K gold bracelet. *$1,750*

Watch courtesy of Skinner Inc.

AUDEMARS PIGUET
- Ultra thin, circa 1970, No. 36989, 18K yellow gold. *$1,800*

Watch courtesy of Heritage Auction Galleries

AUDEMARS PIGUET
- Circa 1960s, 18K white gold, water resistant, screw back, applied bar markers. *$1,850*

Watch courtesy of Heritage Auction Galleries

AUDEMARS PIGUET
- Circa 1985, steel Royal Oak Automatic, stainless steel case, No. 225, polished and brushed finish, back and bezel secured with screws, screw-down crown, anthracite dial, luminous bar hour markers, date at 3, luminous steel batons, white minute marks. *$3,000*

Watch courtesy of Heritage Auction Galleries

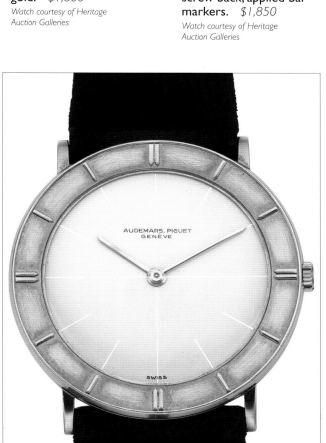

AUDEMARS PIGUET
- Circa 1960s, 18K yellow gold, gold bar markers on the bezel, curved lugs, ultra thin. *$3,000*

Watch courtesy of Heritage Auction Galleries

AUDEMARS PIGUET
- Circa 1950s, 18K yellow gold, stepped bezel, fancy lugs, center seconds, applied gold markers. *$2,000*

Watch courtesy of Heritage Auction Galleries

AUDEMARS PIGUET
- Circa 1940s, platinum, sub seconds, Roman numerals. *$2,250*

Watch courtesy of Heritage Auction Galleries

BAUME ET MERCIER

William Bame

$\mathcal{B}$aume et Mercier, Geneva watch manufacturer, was founded in 1918 by William Baume and Paul Mercier. The venture proved to be a successful one. In 1921, they were awarded the Poincon de Genève, which recognizes companies offering flawless, top-quality merchandise. In 1937 Baume left the company and Mercier retired. The firm continued to operate under the direction of jeweler Constantin de Gorski., and his partner, Robert Peron. In 1965 the firm was acquired by Piaget. Baume et Mercier still operates today, now owned by Cartier.

(Far Left)
BAUME ET MERCIER,
- 18K yellow gold and diamonds, manual wind, 18K yellow gold bracelet.   *$2,500*

Watch courtesy of Heritage Auction Galleries

(Left)
BAUME ET MERCIER
- 18K yellow gold and diamonds, manual wind, 18K yellow gold bracelet.   *$3,500*

Watch courtesy of Heritage Auction Galleries

(Below)
BAUME ET MERCIER
- Platinum and diamond, for Tiffany & Co., manual wind, circa 1930s.   *$3,600*

Watch courtesy of Leslie Hindman Auctioneers

(Above)

BAUME ET MERCIER
- 18K yellow gold and diamonds, manual wind. *$1,300*
  Watch courtesy of Leslie Hindman Auctioneers

(Left)

BAUME ET MERCIER
- 14K white gold and diamonds. *$250*
  Watch courtesy of Leslie Hindman Auctioneers

(Right)

BAUME ET MERCIER
- 14K yellow gold and diamonds, manual wind. *$600*
  Watch courtesy of Heritage Auction Galleries

(Below)

BAUME ET MERCIER
- 14K yellow gold, quartz movement. *$550*
  Watch courtesy of Leslie Hindman Auctioneers

(Left)
BAUME ET MERCIER
- 14K yellow gold and diamonds. *$775*

Watch courtesy of Leslie Hindman Auctioneers

(Top Right)
BAUME ET MERCIER
- Stainless steel, two-register chronograph, circa 1960s. *$1,750*

Watch courtesy of James F. Dicke II

(Right)
BAUME ET MERCIER
- Two time zone, circa 1960s, cushion-shaped case, 18K gold, 29 mm. *$1,200*

Watch courtesy of Heritage Auction Galleries

(Far Right))
BAUME ET MERCIER
- Automatic, circa 1975, 18K yellow gold, synthetic sapphire in crown. *$1,150*

Watch courtesy of Heritage Auction Galleries

BAUME ET MERCIER
- Stainless steel. *$425*

Watch courtesy of Leslie Hindman Auctioneers

BAUME ET MERCIER
- 18K yellow gold, chronograph, circa 1950s *$1,000*

Watch courtesy of Leslie Hindman Auctioneers

BENRUS

*B*enrus was founded in the mid-1920s by Russian immigrant, Benjamin Lazrus. For years prior to opening Benrus, Lazrus repaired watches, and also designed watchbands and watch cases at his shop in New York City. Benrus imported his watch movements from Swiss makers, yet sold them in his American cases as American watches. Benrus also produced two lower-line brands, Sovereign and Belforte. They were also one of the first watch companies to create a waterproof watch.

(Right)
BENRUS
- 14K white gold, manual wind. *$500*

Watch courtesy of Heritage Auction Galleries

(Far Right)
BENRUS
- Platinum, white gold and diamonds, manual wind. *$1,220*

Watch courtesy of Leslie Hindman Auctioneers

(Below)
BENRUS
- 14K yellow gold, teardrop lugs, center second, manual wind, circa 1940s. *$200*

Watch courtesy of Chris Miller

BENRUS
- Wrist alarm, stainless steel. *$225*
  Watch courtesy of Phil Lucas

BENRUS
- Sky Chief Chronograph, 38mm, stainless steel, 17 jewel manual wind, 1940s. *$1,800*
  Watch courtesy of Derek Dier, WatchesToBuy.com

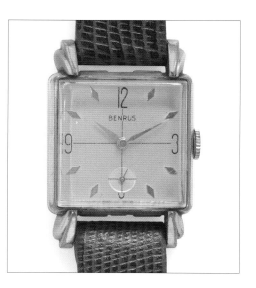

(Above)
BENRUS
- Mother of pearl dial, gold applied numerals, manual wind, 10K yellow gold plated. *$45*
  Watch courtesy of Phil Lucas

(Far Left)
BENRUS
- 14K yellow gold, fancy lugs, sub second, manual wind, circa 1940s. *$200*
  Watch courtesy of Chris Miller

(Left)
BENRUS
- Manual wind, silver dial, gold applied markers, sub second, 10K rose gold plated. *$65*
  Watch courtesy of Tim and Reyne Haines

BLANCPAIN

Jehan-Jacques Blancpain

*B*lancpain was founded in 1735 in a small farmhouse in Switzerland by Jehan-Jacques Blancpain.

Blancpain has always claimed, "Since 1735, there has never been a quartz Blancpain watch." In the 1970s, the desire to keep this promise almost led to the firm's demise. At that time, inexpensive quartz watches were being made in Japan and China. However, with the help of Omega executive, Jean-Claude Biver, they were able to rebuild the brand they were known for, producing fine, limited-edition mechanical watches.

In 1953, Blancpain debuted the famous diver's watch, "Fifty Fathoms." This watch was featured in the award-winning film by Jacques Cousteau, "The World of Silence."

Today, Blancpain produces less than 10,000 watches a year. Each watch is individually numbered and recorded in the company archives. The movements are designed by the firm's sister company. Frederic Piquet. The boxes, buckles and straps are of the highest quality.

The company produces only mechanical, round-case watches. The most recognizable models today are the "Fifty Fathoms" diver's watch, the "Half Hunter," and the "1735" — a six-complication timepiece that includes automatic chronograph, minute repeater, moon phase, perpetual calendar, split-second chronograph and tourbillion.

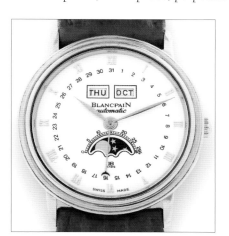

(Top Left)
BLANCPAIN
- Automatic, JB 1735, No. 16, 1980s. Self-winding, water-resistant, stainless steel and 18K pink gold with triple date, moon phases and a stainless steel Blancpain buckle. *$2,500*

Image courtesy of Antiquorum Auctioneers

(Top Right)
BLANCPAIN
- Fifty Fathoms "Aqua Lung 1000 Feet," Ref. 3500, late 1950s. Center-seconds, antimagnetic, self-winding, water-resistant stainless steel, with wide bezel. *$4,500*

Image courtesy of Antiquorum Auctioneers

(Bottom)
BLANCPAIN
- Platinum and diamonds, manual wind with hinged cover. *$11,500*

Watch courtesy of Leslie Hindman Auctioneers

BOREL

Ernest Borel opened his firm in 1856 in Switzerland. This seemingly small watch company was actually quite well known for their chronometers. In 1946, Borel was the second-largest producer of chronometers in the world. They were so well made, they won the Neuchâtel observatory contest in 1866. They continued their success by winning the contest again in 1870, 1875, 1876 and 1890.

ERNEST BOREL
- Cocktail, manual wind, gold plated, circa 1961 (second view shows back). *$150*

Photos courtesy of James F. Dicke II

BOUCHERON

Frédéric Boucheron established his business in France in 1858. Boucheron has always been more than just a fine watch manufacturer. They are also known for their high-profile jewelry. The company is often called "The Jeweler of Time."

Boucheron created a line of lady's bracelet watches in 1880 that started women wearing watches on their wrist as opposed to their lapel.

The popularity of Boucheron jewelry and fine timepieces led to the opening of stores in Moscow in 1898, and in London in 1903.

In 1947, Boucheron launched a new watch called the "Reflet," which offered the wearer the option of interchangeable straps. Today, Boucheron is owned by Gucci.

BOUCHERON
- 18K yellow gold, quartz movement, circa 1970s. *$1,500*

Watch courtesy of James F. Dicke II

(Top Left)
BOUCHERON
- 18K yellow gold,
  quartz movement, circa
  1970s. *$1,500*

  Watch courtesy of James F. Dicke II

(Top Right)
BOUCHERON
- 18K yellow gold,
  quartz movement, circa
  1970s. *$1,500*

  Watch courtesy of James F. Dicke II

(Left)
BOUCHERON
- 18K yellow gold. *$1,200*

  Watch courtesy of Leslie Hindman Auctioneers

BOVET

*T*his maker was founded in London in 1822 by Edouard Bovet, the son of watchmaker Jean-Frederic Bovet. Edouard studied watch making in London in 1814. In 1818, he traveled to China where he sold four of his timepieces for the equivalent of $1 million.

Bovet was best known for their pocket watches manufactured for the Chinese market in the 19th century. Their timepieces were so sought after in China, they contracted with other Swiss manufacturers to help them meet the demand.

Around 1855, the market for watches all but ended for Bovet. The family sold their interest in the company in 1864. However, the new owners continued to produce pocket watches, and would manufacture watches for other watch companies.

In the 1990s, the company began to produce watches again. Some of the Bovet watches produced sell for over $1 million dollars. Bovet produces approximately 2,000 watches a year, many made to order.

BREITLING

*I*n 1884, Leon Breitling formed the Breitling Co. in St. Imier, Switzerland. In the early days, the main goal of Breitling was to create high-quality chronograph watches. He was only 24 years of age at this time.

World War I brought the need for pilot chronographs. In fact, Breitling was the preferred wristwatch of pilots. This same watch became available to the general public, and was called the "Navitimer." In 1942, Breitling introduced the "Chronomat" model. This watch was fitted with a circular slide rule bezel. At this time, the Aircraft Owners and Pilots Association named the three-register version of the "Chronomat" as their official watch. Astronaut Scott Carpenter wore a Breitling into space. That series was named "Cosmonaute."

Like so many other watch companies, times were tough due to quartz movements. To overcome its competition, Breitling hired former pilot Ernest Schneider as its new CEO. It was Schneider's job to market the Breitling name and to change the attitude of the buying public about the bulky watch design.

Over the years, Breitling has created other inventive models such as the "Emergency." This watch will send out a radio signal if the wearer is lost.

Breitling is still in business today, and still makes one of the most desired wristwatches by pilots.

(Top Left)
BREITLING
- "Cosmonaute 1809 Chrono-Matic," circa 1967, stainless steel, screw back, water resistant, round push buttons, automatic. *$2,000*
  Watch courtesy of Heritage Auction Galleries

(Middle Left)
BREITLING
- "Chronomat," Ref. 808, 37mm, stainless steel, manual wind. *$3,450*
  Watch courtesy of Derek Dier, WatchesToBuy.com

(Bottom Left)
BREITLING
- "Navitimer," circa 1967, gold plated, 41mm. *$3,750*
  Watch courtesy of Derek Dier, WatchesToBuy.com

BREITLING
- Genève, "Navitimer," case No. 1146059, Ref. 806, late 1960s. Water-resistant, gold plated and stainless steel with round-button chronograph, registers, tachometer, telemeter and slide-rule. *$2,000*

Image courtesy of Antiquorum Auctioneers

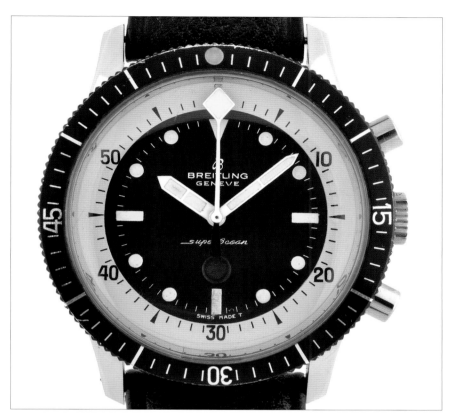

BREITLING
- "Super Ocean," 42.5mm, manual wind, rare, 1960s. *$3,750*

Watch courtesy of Derek Dier, WatchesToBuy.com

BREITLING GENÈVE
- "Top-Time," case No. 1069286, Ref. 810, 1970s. Gold-plated with round-button chronograph, registers and tachometer. *$1,250*

Image courtesy of Antiquorum Auctioneers

BREITLING
- Genève, "Navitimer – Automatic," Ref. 1806, 1970s. Octagonal, self-winding, water-resistant, stainless steel with round-button chronograph, registers, telemeter, slide-rule, date, winding crown at 9 and the chronograph pushers at 2 and 4 o'clock, and a stainless steel Breitling link bracelet. *$3,000*

Image courtesy of Antiquorum Auctioneers

BREITLING
- "Montbrillant Eclipse" chronograph with moon phase, circa 2000, stainless steel, world city locations and time variances on the back, 42 mm, rotating bezel, screw back, water resistant, automatic movement. *$2,400*

Watch courtesy of Heritage Auction Galleries

BREITLING
- Premier Waterproof Chronograph, circa 1950, 18K rose gold, No. 673099, round pushers, antimagnetic, shock protected. *$2,800*

Watch courtesy of Heritage Auction Galleries

BREITLING
- "Chronomat," circa 1989, screw back, stainless steel with gold trim, screw-down crown, water resistant, rotating bezel, automatic movement. *$1,075*

Watch courtesy of Heritage Auction Galleries

BREITLING
- "Unitime" (co-pilot), 41mm, stainless steel, manual wind, 1960s. *$5,000*

Watch courtesy of Derek Dier, WatchesToBuy.com

BREITLING
- "Premier," stainless steel, chronograph, manual wind. *$600*

Watch courtesy of Tim and Reyne Haines

BREITLING
- "Telemetre Dial" chronograph, base metal. *$1,200*

Watch courtesy of Tim and Reyne Haines

BREITLING,
- "Premier" chronograph, manual wind, pink gold. *$2,500*

Watch courtesy of Charlie Cleves - Cleves and Lonnemann Jewelers

BREITLING
- "Datora," automatic moon phase calendar, circa 1950s, 18K rose gold, curved lugs, applied gold markers, moon dial above 6, outer blue date numerals. *$2,500*

Watch courtesy of Heritage Auction Galleries

BREITLING
- GMT, manual wind, Valjoux 72, 40mm, rare, circa 1968. *$7,000*

Watch courtesy of Derek Dier, WatchesToBuy.com

BUCHERER

*B*ucherer was founded in 1888 by Carl F. Bucherer in Lucerne, Switzerland. Bucherer began as a jewelry and watch dealer. His shop was successful and this allowed him to open several stores around Switzerland.

Bucherer watches were made for the wealthy. They combined the best craftsmanship in watch-making along with the finest jewelry-making skills to those who were looking for, and could afford, the best.

Around 1915, Carl's sons, Carl Edouard and Ernst, joined the firm. Ernst was appointed official watchmaker to William II, Kaiser of Germany. Ernst created the first timepiece for the Bucherer brand. At this time, a Bucherer store was opened in Unter den Linden, one of the main streets in Berlin where luxury goods were sold.

Bucherer House has often been compared to Tiffany & Co. Both started as small boutique-type stores and grew to be a strong, recognized brand in their countries.

The Bucherer Co. is still in business today, headed by Jörg Bucherer, the grandson of the original founder. It is privately owned, and has 33 stores throughout Switzerland, Germany and Austria. Bucherer is known for its policy, "Everyone is worth success and luxury life."

(Far Left)
BUCHERER
- **Platinum and diamonds, manual wind.** *$1,500*

  Watch courtesy of Leslie Hindman Auctioneers

(Left)
BUCHERER
- **Automatic chronometer, circa 1960s, 18K yellow gold, smooth bezel, date at 3, black and gold markers, center sweep.** *$300*

  Watch courtesy of Heritage Auction Galleries

BUECHE GIROD

*I*n 1947, Vital Bueche founded Bueche Girod. The company's name combines his last name with that of his wife, Edwige Girod.

Bueche had several patents during his lifetime: 1949, moon-phase wristwatch movement; 1950, plain calendar movement for wristwatches; 1959, musical alarm movement; 1963, movement for a 'Singing Bird' alarm clock.

In the 1950s, Bueche Girod started producing watches and movements for other firms. These were used in Léonidas watches, especially the moon-phase, day/date movements. Roy C. King started a U.K. agency for Bueche Girod in Watford in 1956. In 1958, he started to make watches for Universal Genève.

Bueche Girod also made wristwatches for Bulova.

BUECHE GIROD
- Lady's, circa 1970s, 18K yellow gold, diamond bezel, Roman hour chapters, manual wind, integral 18K yellow gold band. *$1,000*

Watch courtesy of Heritage Auction Galleries

BUECHE GIROD
- Ultra thin, circa 1970s, stepped bezel, curved lugs, 18K yellow gold, black Roman numerals, manual wind, triple signed Bueche Girod. *$600*

Watch courtesy of Heritage Auction Galleries

BUECHE GIROD
- 18K yellow gold and enamel, manual wind, circa 1960. *$1,500*

Watch courtesy of Heritage Auction Galleries

BULOVA

*J*oseph Bulova immigrated to America from Bohemia and opened a jewelry store in New York City in 1875. In 1912, he opened his first factory in Switzerland dedicated to making watch parts. While the movements were produced in Switzerland, the company is still considered an American watch firm.

Their first line of wristwatches didn't hit the market until 1919, and lady's wristwatches became available in 1924.

In 1927, to commemorate the transatlantic flight of Charles Lindbergh from New York to Paris, Bulova created the Lone Eagle wristwatch. They sold 5,000 of these watches within days. It is estimated that more than 50,000 of these watches sold within the next few years.

One of the more recognized Bulova watches, the Accutron, was launched in 1961. The Accutron is known for keeping accurate time within 2 seconds a day. Another unique feature of this watch is its movement: fully electric, not manual wind.

(Right)
BULOVA
- Accutron, gold-filled top, steel back, large tapered lugs, Accutron 214 movement, circa 1960s. *$200*
  Watch courtesy of Heritage Auction Galleries

(Top)
BULOVA
- Accutron, Railroad Approved, circa 1975, offset crown, steel back, gold-plated top, 218 movement. *$200*
  Watch courtesy of Heritage Auction Galleries

(Middle)
BULOVA
- Waterproof, 32mm, stainless steel, 17 jewel manual wind. *$250*
  Watch courtesy of Derek Dier, WatchesToBuy.com

(Bottom)
BULOVA
- Accutron, steel back, gold-plated top, brushed finish to bezel, circa 1975. *$100*
  Watch courtesy of Heritage Auction Galleries

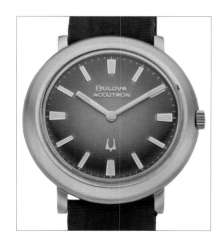

BULOVA
- Manual wind, diamond markers, 10K white gold filled. *$65*

Watch courtesy of Tim and Reyne Haines

BULOVA
- 14K white gold, manual wind, diamond markers, circa 1930s. *$225*

Watch courtesy of Chris Miller

(Above)
BULOVA
- Accutron, Railroad, 36.5mm, stainless steel, electric movement, 1970s. *$800*

Watch courtesy of Derek Dier, WatchesToBuy.com

(Left)
BULOVA
- Accutron, "Deep Sea World Time," stainless steel, circa 1970s. *$1,000*

Watch courtesy of Chris Miller

(Right)
BULOVA
- White gold filled, 21mm, 17 jewel manual wind. *$375*

Watch courtesy of Derek Dier, WatchesToBuy.com

(Right)
BULOVA

- U.S. Military, 30mm, stainless steel, manual wind, 1950s. *$400*

Watch courtesy of Derek Dier, WatchesToBuy.com

(Far Rogjt)
BULOVA

- Stainless steel, military, U.S. Army dedication, black dial, manual wind, white enamel numbers. *$125*

Watch courtesy of Phil Lucas

(Far Left)
BULOVA

- Bullhead Chronograph, 43mm, stainless steel, automatic micro-rotor, 1970s. *$2,500*

Watch courtesy of Derek Dier, WatchesToBuy.com

(Left)
BULOVA

- Automatic, stainless steel, day, circa 1970s. *$125*

Watch courtesy of Phil Lucas

BULOVA
- 14K pink gold, manual wind, sub second, faceted crystal, circa 1940s. *$175*

Watch courtesy of Chris Miller

BULOVA
- Step bezel, gold numerals, sub second, manual wind, 10K yellow gold plated. *$50*

Watch courtesy of Phil Lucas

(Above)
BULOVA
- Exotic gold-filled case, 17 jewel manual wind, 1950s. *$250*

Watch courtesy of Derek Dier, WatchesToBuy.com

(Right)
BULOVA
- 21mm, gold filled, 21 jewel manual, 1940s. *$250*

Watch courtesy of Derek Dier, WatchesToBuy.com

(Bottom Right)
BULOVA
- Manual wind, silver dial, applied gold numbers/markers, sub second, yellow gold filled. *$50*

Watch courtesy of Tim and Reyne Haines

WESTFIELD (BY BULOVA)
- 20.5mm, 17 jewel manual wind. *$495*

Watch courtesy of Derek Dier, WatchesToBuy.com

(Top Left)
BULOVA

- Art Deco, gold filled, 27.5mm, 17 jewel. *$275*

Watch courtesy of Derek Dier, WatchesToBuy.com

(Second from Left)
BULOVA

- 17 jewel manual wind, gold filled, 25mm, 1940s. *$250*

Watch courtesy of Derek Dier, WatchesToBuy.com

(Second from Right)
BULOVA

- Enamel bezel, manual wind, sub second, 14K yellow gold. *$500*

Watch courtesy of Charlie Cleves - Cleves and Lonnemann Jewelers

(Right)
BULOVA

- 10K yellow gold filled, manual wind, circa 1950s. *$150*

Watch courtesy of Leslie Hindman Auctioneers

(Left)
BULOVA

- 25mm, gold filled, 17 jewel manual wind. *$300*

Watch courtesy of Derek Dier, WatchesToBuy.com

BULOVA
- Lady's cocktail, 18.75mm, gold filled, 15 jewel manual wind, 1950s.   *$125*
Watch courtesy of Derek Dier, WatchesToBuy.com

BULOVA
- Oval dial, black Roman numerals, manual wind, 10K rose gold filled.   *$40*
Watch courtesy of Tim and Reyne Haines

BULOVA
- Art Deco, 20mm, gold filled, manual wind, 1940s.   *$400*
Watch courtesy of Derek Dier, WatchesToBuy.com

CARTIER

*C*artier was founded in Paris in 1847 by Louis-Francois Cartier, son of a powder-horn maker.

He quickly made a name for himself selling luxury goods. In 1859 his reputation allowed him to begin selling his wares to the Empress Eugenie. In the same year, Cartier opened a shop in the fashionable area of Boulevard des Italiens to sell his jewelry.

In 1874, Cartier's son, Alfred, took over the business. He expanded the company's product line to include watches. In 1899, Alfred's son, Louis, began working at the firm. Louis had a passion for pocket watches. It was his goal to have pocket watches designed by the firm.

In 1904, Louis Cartier met Brazilian pilot, Alberto Santos-Dumont. Dumont expressed his concern over the lack of reliable pocket watches for aviators. Cartier decided he would design something that would eliminate the problem and thus the "Santos" was born. The "Santos" was a flat wristwatch with a square bezel.

Around 1907, Cartier entered into a partnership with Edmond Jaeger to supply movements for Cartier watches. Cartier also used the movements of other great firms such as Audemars Piguet, LeCoultre, Movado and Vacheron & Constantin.

Some of the Cartier lines we recognize today were made as far back as the early teens. The Baignoire and Tortue models were launched in 1912. The Cartier "Tank" debuted in 1917. Cartier was commissioned by the Pasha of Marrakech to design a waterproof watch. In 1932, the "Pasha" debuted.

In 1942 Louis Cartier died. A group of investors took over in 1972 and named antique dealer, Alain Perrin, as the CEO. Perrin was responsible for the successful "Le Must" line, and for the re-launch of the "Santos" line.

Today, Cartier still produces fine timepieces such as the "Panthere," the "Pasha," the "Tank," and the "Tank Francaise."

Louis-Francois Cartier

(Above)
CARTIER
• 14K yellow gold, manual wind, modern. *$2,300*
Watch courtesy of Heritage Auction Galleries

(Left)
CARTIER
• Santos, stainless steel. *$1,500*
Watch courtesy of Leslie Hindman Auctioneers

CARTIER
- 18K yellow gold, quartz movement, circa 1998. *$1,500*

Watch courtesy of James F. Dicke II

CARTIER
- 18K yellow gold, quartz movement, circa 1970s. *$1,500*

Watch courtesy of James F. Dicke II

CARTIER
- Tank Louis Cartier, 18K white gold, Roman numeral indicators and date aperture, quartz movement. *$4,500*

Watch courtesy of Skinner Inc.

CARTIER
- Tank Louis, 18K gold, Roman numeral indicators. *$1,200*

Watch courtesy of Skinner Inc.

CARTIER/EUROPEAN WATCH & CLOCK. CO.
- France, "Tank Chinoise," 1960s. Square-shaped, 18K yellow gold with an 18K yellow gold Cartier deployant clasp. Accompanied by a fitted Cartier box. *$15,000*

Image courtesy of Antiquorum Auctioneers

(Right)
CARTIER
- "Roadster," stainless steel, automatic, contemporary. *$1,500*
  Watch courtesy of James F. Dicke II

(Below)
CARTIER/EUROPEAN WATCH & CLOCK CO.
- Case No. 420171, 1155. Movement No. 420474, 1930s, 18K gold square-hinged case with contemporary gold-plated Cartier buckle *$2,000*
  Image courtesy of Antiquorum Auctioneers

(Bottom)
CARTIER
- Lady's, Centiure, circa 1970s, 18K yellow gold, black Roman numerals, manual wind. *$800*
  Watch courtesy of Heritage Auction Galleries

(Above)
CARTIER/CONCORD
- 14K gold, Roman numeral indicators, enclosing Concord 17-jewel movement, circa 1950s. *$450*
  Watch courtesy of Skinner Inc.

(Left)
CARTIER
- Paris, No. 782580129, 1980s. Cushion-shaped, 18K yellow gold lady's with an 18K yellow gold Cartier buckle. *$1,500*
  Image courtesy of Antiquorum Auctioneers

CARTIER
- Tank American, lady's, 18K white gold and diamonds, Roman numeral indicators, bracelet with deployant clasp, diamond melee, quartz movement. *$25,000*
  Watch courtesy of Skinner Inc.

(Above)
CARTIER
• Tank Francaise, two-tone. *$2,600*

Watch courtesy of Leslie Hindman Auctioneers

(Right)
CARTIER/EUROPEAN
WATCH & CLOCK CO.
• Circa 1920s, Art Deco, 18K yellow gold, Roman numerals, back wind and back set, signed Cartier France on the dial, European Watch & Clock Co. on the movement. *$6,000*

Watch courtesy of Heritage Auction Galleries

(Below)
CARTIER
• Lady's, hexagonal "Santos," 18K and stainless steel, automatic. *$1,400*

Watch courtesy of Charlie Cleves - Cleves and Lonnemann Jewelers

(Above)
CARTIER
• Santos, stainless steel, Roman numeral indicators, automatic, polished bezel. *$1,000*

Watch courtesy of Skinner Inc.

(Below)
CARTIER
• Lady's, Tank Francaise, circa 2003, stainless steel, sapphire set crown, No. 447642CE, Ref. 2384. *$2,000*

Watch courtesy of Heritage Auction Galleries

CARTIER
• Panthere, 18K yellow gold quartz movement, box/papers. *$5,500*
Watch courtesy of Leslie Hindman Auctioneers

CARTIER
• Tank, 18K gold, Roman numeral indicators, bracelet, original presentation box. *$6,000*
Watch courtesy of Skinner Inc.

CARTIER
• Tank Francaise, 18K gold, white dial with Roman numeral indicators and date aperture, automatic. *$5,000*
Watch courtesy of Skinner Inc.

CHOPARD

*I*n 1860, at the age of 24, Louis-Ulysse Chopard opened his first watch making business. There were numerous Swiss watchmakers offering fine timepieces at this time. Chopard knew he needed to do something to make his work stand out above the rest. His slogan was, "Quality with the maximum possible work by hand."

That motto would pay off over the next 150 years. Chopard became well known in Scandinavia and Eastern Europe. By the 1930s, the firm had expanded to a staff of 150.

Today, Chopard is alive and well in Geneva, still recognized for their luxury brand of wristwatches, and employs more than 700 people across Switzerland.

(Above)
CHOPARD
- Lady's, circa 1970, 18K yellow gold, angled lugs, black batons, manual wind, dial also signed Tiffany & Co. *$650*
Watch courtesy of Heritage Auction Galleries

(Left)
CHOPARD
- Luna D'Oro Moon Phase for Tiffany & Co., modern, 18K yellow gold, model 1086, water resistant, stepped bezel, down-turned lugs, quartz movement. *$1,200*
Watch courtesy of Heritage Auction Galleries

(Below)
CHOPARD
- "Happy," 18K yellow gold and diamonds, manual wind. *$3,400*
Watch courtesy of Leslie Hindman Auctioneers

CHRONOGRAPHE SUISSE

*W*atches marked *"Chronographe Suisse" were made during the 1940s through the late 1950s. They were generic Swiss watches made for the tourist trade. The cases were made of an exterior of sheet gold and an inner case made of heavy brass.*

An interesting note: They were commonly made with cheap Landeron movements. Their life expectancy was a mere 14 days; enough time for the tourists to return home. However, many of them have survived and are still running strong today.

CHRONOGRAPHE SUISSE
• 18K gold, 17 jewel manual wind, circa 1943.   *$1,450*
Watch courtesy of Derek Dier, WatchesToBuy.com

CONCORD

oncord was founded in Bienne, Switzerland, in 1908. From the beginning, Concord has been recognized for its line of luxury timepieces using platinum, diamonds, emeralds, rubies and sapphires.

Concord is not only recognized for their quality wristwatches, but also for their clock designs. They are best known for their "Ring Clock" which was the first portable eight-day winding travel alarm clock.

Concord is still producing top-of-the-line watches today.

(Top Far Left)
CONCORD
- 18K yellow gold and diamond bezel, quartz movement, 18K yellow gold bracelet, *$1,000*
  Watch courtesy of Heritage Auction Galleries

(Middle Far Left)
CONCORD
- 18K yellow gold and diamonds, quartz movement, circa 1980. *$1,200*
  Watch courtesy of Heritage Auction Galleries

(Left)
CONCORD
- 18K yellow gold, quartz, circa 1970s. *$2,500*
  Watch courtesy of James F. Dicke II

(Bottom)
CONCORD
- 14K yellow gold and diamonds. *$500*
  Watch courtesy of Leslie Hindman Auctioneers

CONCORD
- Day/night dual time, circa 1970, 14K yellow gold, cushion shape, teardrop lugs, black dial with gold leaf hands, Roman numerals, manual wind. *$500*

  Watch courtesy of Heritage Auction Galleries

CONCORD
- Acapulco 666, automatic, circa 1970, stainless steel, screw back, day and date, bar markers. *$150*

  Watch courtesy of Heritage Auction Galleries

CONCORD
- 14K yellow gold, water resistant, gold and luminescent "lance" hands, center sweep, automatic, circa 1960. *$175*

  Watch courtesy of Heritage Auction Galleries

CONCORD
- "Saratoga," lady's, 18K gold and diamonds, Roman numeral indicators, quartz movement, diamond melee bezel. *$1,500*

  Watch courtesy of Skinner Inc.

CORUM

orum was founded in 1955 at La Chaux-de-Fonds, Switzerland, by Simone Ries and Rene Bannwart. From the beginning, Corum made a mark in the watch industry by creating the $20 Liberty Eagle watch. This watch was made from a genuine U.S. $20 gold coin.

Some of the other more recognizable Corum watches are the "Romulus," the "Golden Bridge" and the "Admiral's Cup."

Corum created the popular "Bubble Watch" along with the "Rolls Royce" watch (complete with grill and hood ornament). Corum is still creating fine timepieces today, such as a minute repeater and a minute repeater/tourbillon.

(Above)
CORUM
• 18K yellow gold and diamonds, Rolls-Royce "Spirit of Ecstasy," manual wind, circa 1985. *$5,000*
Watch courtesy of Heritage Auction Galleries

(Left)
CORUM
• "Golden Bridge," 18K white gold, skeletonized back, pavé diamond lugs, double row of diamonds top and bottom, sapphire crystals, manual wind, circa 2006. *$9,850*
Watch courtesy of Heritage Auction Galleries

(Top Left)
CORUM
- Bubble "Golf," sapphire crystal, No. 662003, water resistant, screw-down crown, quartz movement, circa 2005. *$800*
  Watch courtesy of Heritage Auction Galleries

(Top Middle)
CORUM
- 18K yellow gold, sweep second hand. *$800*
  Watch courtesy of Heritage Auction Galleries

(Top Right)
CORUM
- 18K yellow gold, applied gold bar markers, gold batons, center seconds sweep, automatic, dial also signed "for Paul Breguette," circa 1960. *$1,000*
  Watch courtesy of Heritage Auction Galleries

CORUM
- 18K yellow gold, stepped bezel, quartz, circa 1980s. *$400*
  Watch courtesy of Heritage Auction Galleries

CORUM
- $20 gold coin cover, 18K yellow gold, manual wind, circa 1975. *$2,500*
  Watch courtesy of Heritage Auction Galleries

CORUM
- 18K yellow gold, manual wind. *$1,450*

Watch courtesy of Leslie Hindman Auctioneers

CORUM
- No. 438, rectangular, 18K yellow gold and diamond made of a 15-gram 999.9 gold ingot, circa 1975. *$1,250*

Image courtesy of Antiquorum Auctioneers

(Above)
CORUM
- $10 Dollar gold coin, modern, 18K gold lugs and sides, diamond set crown, 30 mm, sapphire crystal. *$1,900*

Watch courtesy of Heritage Auction Galleries

(Top Right)
CORUM
- 1893 $10 Liberty coin, 18K/22k gold, diamond-set crown, hour marks on the bezel, quartz, circa 1980s. *$1,800*

Watch courtesy of Heritage Auction Galleries

(Top Left)
CORUM
- $10 gold Liberty Eagle, 28.5mm, 18 jewel manual wind. *$2,950*

Watch courtesy of Derek Dier, WatchesToBuy.com

CROTON

The history of Croton begins more than 130 years ago. Croton was known for quality at an affordable price. Not only was it affordable, Croton felt so strongly about the quality of their timepieces, they offered a lifetime warranty on all of their movements.

Croton is still in production today, and a strong seller with the public. Croton has also managed to capture the attention of celebrities such as Josh Groban, Quincy Jones, Taylor Swift and Miley Cyrus.

(Above)
CROTON
- Nivada Grenchen, 18K white gold, sub seconds, gold bar markers, manual wind, circa 1960s. *$175*

Watch courtesy of Heritage Auction Galleries

(Right)
CROTON
- 14K yellow gold, hinged diamond-ornamented cover, mother-of pearl dial, manual wind, 14K gold band, circa 1940s. *$1,250*

Watch courtesy of Heritage Auction Galleries

(Right)
CROTON
- Lady's, manual wind, 14K white gold with diamonds. *$600*

Watch courtesy of Charlie Cleves - Cleves and Lonnemann Jewelers

PAUL DITISHEIM

*P*aul Ditisheim was a watchmaker at an early age. At the age of 13 he received a diploma from the Horological School of La Chaux-de-Fonds. He then worked for several major watchmakers including his father's firm, Vulcain, until 1892.

It was at that time he established to companies, Solvil and Titus. Many of the watches under the Solvil brand were signed Paul Ditisheim.

The most desirable Ditisheim watches are the Art Deco designs in platinum and diamonds, produced during the 1920s - 1930s. Ditisheim died in 1945.

TITUS
- Chronograph, 18K rose gold, 37.5mm, 17 jewel manual wind. *$1,250*
  Watch courtesy of Derek Dier, WatchesToBuy.com

PAUL DITISHEIM
- 14K pink gold, rubies and diamonds, manual wind, circa 1930. *$1,500*
  Watch courtesy of Heritage Auction Galleries

DOXA

oxa opened their doors in 1889 in Switzerland. Founder Georges Ducommun had his first taste of the watch industry when he became an apprentice at a watch movement company at the age of 12. By the time he was 20 years old, he had opened his own watch repair shop.

In the 1930s, watchmakers were challenged to manufacturer dashboard timepieces for racecars. Doxa chose their high-grade, eight-day watch movement, which found a home with automobile and racecar manufacturer; Bugatti.

DOXA
• Le Locle, chronograph, antimagnetic, case No. 4815380, circa 1950. Stainless steel with square button chronograph, register, tachometer and telemeter. *$1,250*
Image courtesy of Antiquorum Auctioneers

DOXA
• Triple-calendar chronograph, 14K yellow gold, 1946 U.S. Army Engineers A.P.O. inscription, gold Arabic numerals, day and month, 30-minute register, manual wind, original box. *$1,000*
Watch courtesy of Heritage Auction Galleries

DOXA
• 14K yellow gold, gold bar markers, center sweep, manual wind, circa 1960. *$150*
Watch courtesy of Heritage Auction Galleries

DOXA
• 18K pink gold, extended lugs, manual wind, circa 1960. *$250*
Watch courtesy of Heritage Auction Galleries

EBEL

*I*n 1911, Eugène Blum and Alice Lèvy registered the Ebel watch brand with the Chamber of Commerce in La Chaux-de-Fonds, Switzerland. Their first line of watches hit the marketplace in 1912.

Ebel won a gold medal at the Swiss National Exhibition for their ring watches with escapement and hidden time-setting movements. This created a market for Ebel to produce complete timepieces to be branded under other watchmakers' names. Makers such as Vacheron & Constantin, Cartier and Paul Breguette were clients of Ebel.

The brand "Paul Breguette" was created by Ebel for the American market in around 1929. Ebel is still in production today.

(Top Left)
PAUL BREGUETTE
• 14K white gold and diamonds, manual wind. *$400*
Watch courtesy of Leslie Hindman Auctioneers

(Bottom Left)
EBEL
• Automatic, calendar, three-register chronograph, 18K yellow gold and stainless steel. *$2,200*
Watch courtesy of Charlie Cleves - Cleves and Lonnemann Jewelers

(Top Right)
EBEL
• Lady's, mother of pearl dial, two tone, quartz movement. *$1,000*
Watch courtesy of Charlie Cleves - Cleves and Lonnemann Jewelers

(Bottom Right)
EBEL
• Lady's Beluga, 18K yellow gold, double row of diamonds on each side, water resistant, quartz movement, circa 2000. *$2,400*
Watch courtesy of Heritage Auction Galleries

EBERHARD

*E*berhard is a brand known for its connection to the racing world. Founded in Switzerland in 1887, Eberhard was named the office timepiece of the first European car race. Eberhard never lost their passion for racing. In 1992 they created a chronograph, the "Tazio Nuvolari," named after the Italian race car driver.

As with other makers in the 30s, Eberhard began producing watches for the military. They were the official timepiece for the Italian Navy. In 1939 they created a chronograph with the Rattrapante system to perform dual chronometry.

EBERHARD
- Single-button chronograph, 18K yellow gold, wire lugs, hinged case back, No. 17660, signed EB & Co., circa 1910. *$1,600*
Watch courtesy of Heritage Auction Galleries

ELGIN

*T*he firm was founded in 1864 in Elgin, Ill., as the National Watch Co. In the early days, Elgin was best known for its pocket-watch movements.

In 1874, the company changed its name to the Elgin National Watch Co. They ceased operation in the 1960s. Elgin watches are readily available on the market, and often quite affordable.

ELGIN
• Lady Tiger, 14K white gold with enamel inlay, 17mm, manual wind, circa 1928. *$5,000*

Watch courtesy of Derek Dier, WatchesToBuy.com

ELGIN
• 22mm, gold filled with enamel inset, 17 jewel manual wind. *$400*

Watch courtesy of Derek Dier, WatchesToBuy.com

LORD ELGIN
• 14K gold filled, hinged lugs, manual wind, circa 1940s. *$75*

Watch courtesy of Chris Miller

ELGIN
• Anniversary Model, circa 1951, 18K gold, hinged oversize hooded lugs, No. 1024105. *$1,550*

Watch courtesy of Heritage Auction Galleries

ELGIN
• 14K white gold and diamonds, manual wind. *$350*

Watch courtesy of Heritage Auction Galleries

LORD ELGIN
- Manual wind, sub second, 14K yellow gold filled, circa 1941. *$45*

Watch courtesy of Phil Lucas

LORD ELGIN
- 14K yellow gold filled, manual wind, sub second, circa 1940s. *$50*

Watch courtesy of Chris Miller

ELGIN
- U.S. Military, in sterling silver with enamel dial, circa 1920s. *$325*

Watch courtesy of Tim and Reyne Haines

ELGIN
- Silver dial, gold numerals, sub second, rose gold plated and base metal back, manual wind. *$45*

Watch courtesy of Tim and Reyne Haines

ELGIN
- Stepped case, manual wind, applied numeric hour markers, circa 1930s. *$225*

Watch courtesy of Tim and Reyne Haines

ELGIN
- Automatic, square case with round dial, screw back in polished stainless steel, circa 1950s. *$225*

Watch courtesy of Tim and Reyne Haines

ELGIN
- Rectangular dial, manual wind, sub second, yellow gold plated. *$40*

Watch courtesy of Tim and Reyne Haines

ELGIN
- "Golf Ball," manual wind, 10K rose gold plated. *$125*

Watch courtesy of Tim and Reyne Haines

ETERNA

*T*his *company was originally founded in Grenchen, Switzerland, by physician Josef Gerard and teacher Urs Schild as a means to alleviate unemployment in that region. Originally, they produced movements for pocket watches and eventually producing complete watches.*

Eterna had worked on alarms for pocket watches, and were responsible for creating the first wristwatch alarm. They are also known for these firsts:

1962, The Eterna-Matic 3000, the thinnest automatic wristwatch for men.

1976, The Royal Quartz Kon-Tiki, the thinnest quartz watch.

1979, smallest water-resistant quartz watch.

1980, The Museum, the thinnest watch ever produced.

In 1947, Thor Heyerdahl wore an Eterna wristwatch on the 4,300-mile voyage across the Pacific Ocean aboard the Kon-Tiki. The watch continued to operate during and after the journey without a glitch. Eterna decided to name their sports watches "Kon-Tiki" after this journey.

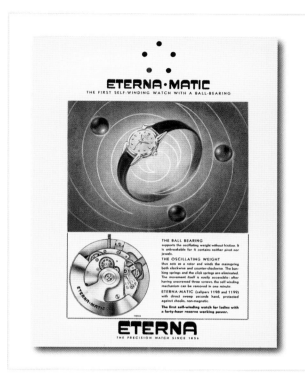

(Left Top)
ETERNA
- 14K yellow gold, manual wind, circa 1940s.   *$225*

Watch courtesy of Chris Miller

(Left Bottom)
ETERNA-MATIC
- Gray dial, bar markers, stainless steel, 1000.   *$150*

Watch courtesy of Leslie Hindman Auctioneers

(Rigjht Top)
ETERNA-MATIC
- 14K yellow gold, chronometer.   *$850*

Watch courtesy of Leslie Hindman Auctioneers

(Right Bottom)
ETERNA-MATIC
- 30mm, stainless steel hourglass case, automatic, 1960s.   *$950*

Watch courtesy of Derek Dier, WatchesToBuy.com

GALLET

*O*riginally known for producing pocket-watch cases and necklace watches for women, Gallet soon became known as the first manufacturer of wristwatches for men and women in 1895.

In 1916, they were the world's first supplier of chronograph wristwatches to the British Army. During World War II, they were supplying watches to the British, American and Canadian armies.

Should your travels call for a visit to the International Museum of Watches in La Chaux-de-Fonds, you will find an important collection of Gallet watches on view, donated by the Gallet family.

GALLET
- "Up Down" single-button chronograph in stainless steel. *$450*

Watch courtesy of Chris Miller

GIRARD-PERREGAUX

*C*ontantin Girard and his wife, Marie Perregaux, married in 1854 and took over the business of Geneva watch manufacturer, Jean-Francois Bautte, in 1856.

Constantin Girard was an important watchmaker. One of his masterpieces, the "Tourbillon Sous Trois Points d'Or" (Tourbillon with Three Gold Bridges) won two gold medals at the Paris Universal Exhibition, in 1867 and 1889.

Girard-Perregaux was known for its innovation. They were the first company to step away from pocket watches and design a full series of watches to be worn on the wrist around 1880.

Though famous for mechanical movements, Girard-Perregaux designed top-quality quartz movements during the 1970s when many other watch companies floundered.

In the early 1990s, Girard-Perregaux joined with Italian carmaker Ferrari to create a line of chronographs that have become highly collectible today. Also during this time, the firm used the technology from the Tourbillon Sous Trois Points d'Or in a wristwatch. The watch was completely handmade, and took six to eight months to complete.

(Above)
GIRARD-PERREGAUX
• Lady's, 14K white gold, white gold bracelet, diamond bezel, manual wind, circa 1950. *$195*
Watch courtesy of Heritage Auction Galleries

(Far Left)
GIRARD-PERREGAUX
• Modern, stainless steel, brushed finish to bezel, transparent sapphire back, automatic movement. *$2,300*
Watch courtesy of Heritage Auction Galleries

(Left)
GIRARD-PERREGAUX
• Richeville chronograph, No. 258, Ref. 2765. Made in a limited series since 1992. Tonneau-shaped, self-winding, water-resistant, 18K pink gold with oval button chronograph, registers, date and an 18K pink gold Girard-Perregaux deployant clasp. Accompanied by an oval leather case. *$3,000*
Image courtesy of Antiquorum Auctioneers

GIRARD-PERREGAUX
- 14K gold and diamonds, diamond case, with mesh bracelet. *$700*

  Watch courtesy of Skinner Inc.

GIRARD PERREGAUX
- Stainless steel, sub second. *$250*

  Watch courtesy of Leslie Hindman Auctioneers

GIRARD PERREGAUX
- Stainless steel, sub second, manual wind. *$225*

  Watch courtesy of Leslie Hindman Auctioneers

GIRARD PERREGAUX
- 10K yellow gold filled, sweep second, manual wind. *$100*

  Watch courtesy of Leslie Hindman Auctioneers

GIRARD-PERREGAUX
- 18K yellow gold, manual wind. *$335*

  Watch courtesy of Leslie Hindman Auctioneers

GLYCINE

*G*lycine was founded in Bienne, Switzerland, in 1914 by Eugène Meylan.

Meylan brought a meticulous attention to detail. He was best known for his small movements used in lady's watches cased in gold and platinum, and often adorned with diamonds. Meylan considered his watches works of art, and began supplying these works to the wealthy.

The Great Depression greatly affected the watch-making community. However, Glycine managed to not only survive but to thrive in these hard times and exhibited at the Basel Fair in 1938 – a fair they have continued to exhibit at ever since.

(Far Left)
GLYCINE
- **14K yellow gold, white gold and diamonds.** *$475*

Watch courtesy of Leslie Hindman Auctioneers

(Left)
GLYCINE
- **Lady's, manual wind, platinum with diamonds** *$1,000*

*Watch courtesy of Charlie Cleves
- Cleves and Lonnemann Jewelers*

GRUEN

Dietrich Gruen

*G*ruen, (originally named D. Gruen and Son was founded in 1894 by Fred and Dietrich Gruen in Columbus, Ohio.

This was not their first venture in watch making. In 1876, Dietrich Gruen, in a partnership with W.J. Savage, formed the Columbus Watch Manufacturing Co. The company, over time, had several partners, which eventually became problematic for Dietrich and Fred, who decided to leave the firm in 1894. Dietrich, along with his son, Frederick, went on to form D. Gruen & Son. A few years later, another son joined the firm and the company name changed to D. Gruen & Sons. In the early 1900s, the name was changed a final time to just Gruen.

In 1903, Gruen introduced its "Veri-Thin" line of watches. By 1908 they were producing both men's and lady's wristwatches. At first, their line of wristwatches were more popular with women than with men.

Dietrich Gruen died in 1911 and son Fredrick took control of the company. He decided to move the business to Cincinnati in 1917.

One of the most recognized lines of Gruen watches, the "Curvex," was introduced in 1935.

After the passing of Fred Gruen and his son, George, the remaining family sold their interest in the company. Gruen Watch Co. was deeply in debt by 1958, and began laying off employees. Gruen's Cincinnati location closed and moved to New York. The company closed their doors permanently in 1976.

(Left)
GRUEN
- Precision, fancy lugs, diamond markers, 14K yellow gold. *$700*
Watch courtesy of Charlie Cleves - Cleves and Lonnemann Jewelers

(Top Right)
GRUEN
- Precision "Airflight," manual wind, circa 1960s, yellow gold filled. *$500*
Watch courtesy of Charlie Cleves - Cleves and Lonnemann Jewelers

(Bottom Right)
GRUEN
- "Mystery Dial," fancy lugs, automatic, 14K yellow gold. *$500*
Watch courtesy of Charlie Cleves - Cleves and Lonnemann Jewelers

GRUEN
- Early diver's, sterling case, manual wind, luminescent numbers. *$600*

Watch courtesy of Charlie Cleves - Cleves and Lonnemann Jewelers

(Top Left)
GRUEN
- "Continental" auto-wind, skeleton back, yellow gold filled. *$250*

Watch courtesy of Charlie Cleves - Cleves and Lonnemann Jewelers

(Top Middle)
GRUEN
- Precision, auto-wind, smooth Roman numeral bezel, stainless steel, skeleton back. *$200*

Watch courtesy of Charlie Cleves - Cleves and Lonnemann Jewelers

(Top Right)
GRUEN
- Precision, stainless steel, chronograph, manual wind. *$350*

Watch courtesy of Leslie Hindman Auctioneers

GRUEN
- Veri-Thin Precision, pink gold filled and stainless steel, 24-hour dial, fancy lugs. *$250*

Watch courtesy of Charlie Cleves - Cleves and Lonnemann Jewelers

GRUEN

- Precision alarm,
  stainless steel. *$200*

*Watch courtesy of Charlie Cleves
- Cleves and Lonnemann Jewelers*

GRUEN

- Veri-Thin, 24 hour, 14K
  yellow gold, manual wind,
  circa 1940s. *$225*

Watch courtesy of Chris Miller

GRUEN

- Veri-Thin Precision, 24 hour dial,
  fancy lugs, 14K pink gold. *$450*

Watch courtesy of Charlie Cleves - Cleves and Lonnemann Jewelers

GRUEN

- Veri-Thin Precision, 24-hour dial, manual
  wind, 10K yellow gold filled. *$250*

Watch courtesy of Charlie Cleves - Cleves and Lonnemann Jewelers

GRUEN

- Veri-Thin Precision, 24-
  hour dial, manual wind,
  stainless steel. *$150*

*Watch courtesy of Charlie Cleves
- Cleves and Lonnemann Jewelers*

GRUEN

- Veri-Thin Precision, 24
  hour dial, fancy lugs,
  yellow gold filled. *$150*

*Watch courtesy of Charlie Cleves
- Cleves and Lonnemann Jewelers*

GRUEN

- Veri-Thin Precision, 24-hour dial, manual
  wind, 10K pink gold filled. *$275*

Watch .courtesy of Charlie Cleves - Cleves and Lonnemann Jewelers

(Right)
GRUEN
- Early military, luminescent numbers, sub second, porcelain dial. *$250*

Watch courtesy of Charlie Cleves - Cleves and Lonnemann Jewelers

(Far Top Right)
GRUEN
- Precision, diver's, stainless steel, circa 1970s. *$100*

Watch courtesy of Charlie Cleves - Cleves and Lonnemann Jewelers

(Far Right)
GRUEN
- Enamel bezel, manual wind, faceted crystal, chrome plated. *$200*

Watch courtesy of Charlie Cleves - Cleves and Lonnemann Jewelers

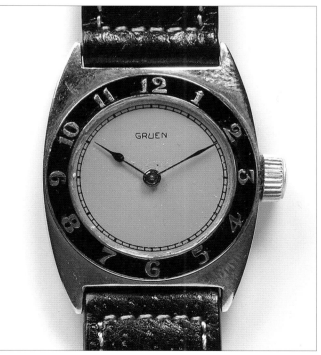

GRUEN
- Precision "21," manual wind, 10K yellow gold filled. *$200*

Watch courtesy of Charlie Cleves - Cleves and Lonnemann Jewelers

GRUEN
- Precision "21," manual wind, 10K white gold filled. *$200*

Watch courtesy of Charlie Cleves - Cleves and Lonnemann Jewelers

GRUEN
- Enamel bezel, manual wind, 14K white gold. *$900*

Watch courtesy of Charlie Cleves - Cleves and Lonnemann Jewelers

GRUEN
- Manual wind, Art Deco case, black enamel numerals, 18K white gold. *$1,200*
Watch courtesy of Charlie Cleves - Cleves and Lonnemann Jewelers

GRUEN
- Precision, fancy lugs, black dial, diamond markers, manual wind, 10K gold filled. *$200*
Watch courtesy of Charlie Cleves - Cleves and Lonnemann Jewelers

GRUEN
- Veri-Thin, 26mm, gold filled, 17 jewel manual wind. *$250*
Watch courtesy of Derek Dier, WatchesToBuy.com

(Above)
GRUEN
- Curved, 20mm, 15 jewel gold-filled manual wind. *$450*
Watch courtesy of Derek Dier, WatchesToBuy.com

(Top Right)
GRUEN
- Curvex, long case, manual wind, 10K yellow gold filled, 46mm. *$300*
Watch courtesy of Charlie Cleves - Cleves and Lonnemann Jewelers

(Right)
GRUEN
- 10K yellow gold filled, manual wind. *$300*
Watch courtesy of Leslie Hindman Auctioneers

(Far Right)
GRUEN
- 14K gold filled, manual wind. *$75*
Watch courtesy of Leslie Hindman Auctioneers

GRUEN
• Veri-Thin Precision, 24-hour dial, 10K yellow gold filled. *$200*

Watch courtesy of Charlie Cleves - Cleves and Lonnemann Jewelers

GRUEN
• Manual wind, 14K white gold, pink gold and silver dial. *$250*

Watch courtesy of Charlie Cleves - Cleves and Lonnemann Jewelers

GRUEN
• Veri-Thin Precision, manual wind, 10K yellow gold filled. *$250*

Watch courtesy of Charlie Cleves - Cleves and Lonnemann Jewelers

GRUEN
• Precision, diamond bezel, manual wind, 10K white gold filled. *$250*

Watch courtesy of Charlie Cleves - Cleves and Lonnemann Jewelers

GRUEN
• Curvex, flexible "bat wing" lugs, gold filled, 21mm, 1940s. *$1,800*

Watch courtesy of Derek Dier, WatchesToBuy.com

GRUEN
• Curvex, driver's, black dial, flex lugs, 10K gold filled. *$1,100*

Watch courtesy of Charlie Cleves - Cleves and Lonnemann Jewelers

(Above)
GRUEN
• Veri-Thin, center sub second, pink gold and
  sterling back, manual wind.   *$400*
  Watch courtesy of Charlie Cleves - Cleves and Lonnemann Jewelers

(Right)
GRUEN
• Veri-Thin, center sub second, square,
  manual wind, yellow gold.   *$350*
  Watch courtesy of Charlie Cleves - Cleves and Lonnemann Jewelers

(Far Right)
GRUEN
• Veri-Thin, center sub second, manual wind,
  yellow gold and sterling back.   *$350*
  Watch courtesy of Charlie Cleves - Cleves and Lonnemann Jewelers

(Far Left)
GRUEN
- Veri-Thin Precision, center sub second, manual wind, yellow gold plated.   *$350*
  Watch courtesy of Charlie Cleves - Cleves and Lonnemann Jewelers

(Left)
GRUEN
- Veri-Thin, manual wind, center sub second, yellow gold.   *$500*
  Watch courtesy of Charlie Cleves - Cleves and Lonnemann Jewelers

(Below)
GRUEN
- Veri-Thin Precision, center sub second, manual wind, yellow gold plated.   *$350*
  Watch courtesy of Charlie Cleves - Cleves and Lonnemann Jewelers

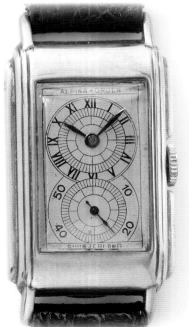

(Above)
GRUEN
- Doctor's, 877 movement, duo dial, manual wind, sterling silver. *$5,000*
  Watch courtesy of Charlie Cleves - Cleves and Lonnemann Jewelers

(Top Left)
GRUEN
- Doctor's, 877 movement, duo dial, jump hour, sterling silver, circa 1930s. *$6,000*
  Watch courtesy of Charlie Cleves - Cleves and Lonnemann Jewelers

(Left)
GRUEN
- "Alpina," doctor's, 877 movement, duo dial, blue enamel, Roman numerals, manual wind, sterling silver. *$4,000*
  Watch courtesy of Charlie Cleves - Cleves and Lonnemann Jewelers

(Right)
GRUEN
- Doctor's, fancy Deco dial, 877 movement, manual wind, yellow gold.   *$2,000*
  Watch courtesy of Charlie Cleves - Cleves and Lonnemann Jewelers

(Bottom Left)
GRUEN
- Doctor's, 877 movement, duo dial, black enamel Roman numerals, manual wind, 14K white gold filled.   *$3,000*
  Watch courtesy of Charlie Cleves - Cleves and Lonnemann Jewelers

(Bottom Middle)
GRUEN
- Doctor's, manual wind, 877 movement, stainless steel.   *$2,000*
  Watch courtesy of Charlie Cleves - Cleves and Lonnemann Jewelers

(Bottom Right)
GRUEN
- Doctor's, silver dial, black enamel numbers, manual wind, stainless steel, caliber 690 movement.   *$1,200*
  Watch courtesy of Charlie Cleves - Cleves and Lonnemann Jewelers

(Right Second from Bottom)
GRUEN
- Doctor's, 10K yellow gold filled, 500 movement, manual wind.   *$1,500*
  Watch courtesy of Charlie Cleves - Cleves and Lonnemann Jewelers

GRUEN
- Precision, Art Deco bezel, sub second, manual wind, 14K white gold. *$900*
Watch courtesy of Charlie Cleves - Cleves and Lonnemann Jewelers

(Left)
GRUEN
- Curvex, manual wind, 10K white gold filled, 42mm. *$350*
Watch courtesy of Charlie Cleves - Cleves and Lonnemann Jewelers

(Below)
GRUEN
- Curvex, manual wind, 10K yellow gold filled, 42mm. *$250*
Watch courtesy of Charlie Cleves - Cleves and Lonnemann Jewelers

GRUEN
- Curvex, manual wind, stainless steel, 44mm. *$900*
Watch courtesy of Charlie Cleves - Cleves and Lonnemann Jewelers

(Above)
GRUEN
- Curvex, manual wind, faceted crystal, 10K white gold filled, 42mm. *$300*
Watch courtesy of Charlie Cleves - Cleves and Lonnemann Jewelers

(Right)
GRUEN
- Curvex, manual wind, faceted crystal, 10K yellow gold filled, 42mm. *$300*
Watch courtesy of Charlie Cleves - Cleves and Lonnemann Jewelers

(Right)
'GRUEN
- Curvex, 10K yellow gold filled, 41mm, manual wind, circa 1940s. *$225*

Watch courtesy of Chris Miller

(Below)
GRUEN
- Curvex, faceted crystal, manual wind, 10K yellow gold filled, 43mm. *$300*

Watch courtesy of Charlie Cleves - Cleves and Lonnemann Jewelers

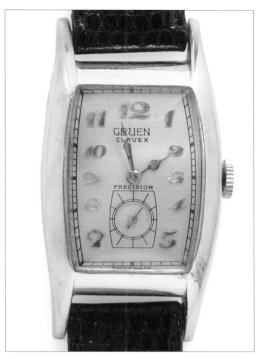

GRUEN
- Curvex, manual wind, platinum, 41mm. *$3,500*

Watch courtesy of Charlie Cleves - Cleves and Lonnemann Jewelers

(Above)
GRUEN
- Curvex, manual wind, 10K yellow gold filled, 42mm. *$200*

Watch courtesy of Charlie Cleves - Cleves and Lonnemann Jewelers

(Left)
GRUEN
- Curvex, faceted crystal, manual wind, 10K yellow gold, 42mm. *$250*

Watch courtesy of Charlie Cleves - Cleves and Lonnemann Jewelers

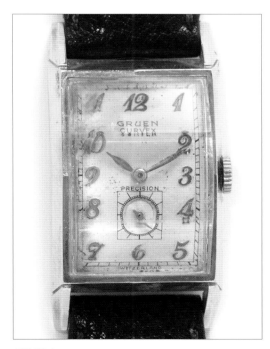

GRUEN
- Curvex, manual wind, 14K yellow gold, faceted crystal, 41mm. *$500*

Watch courtesy of Charlie Cleves - Cleves and Lonnemann Jewelers

(Left)

GRUEN

- Curvex, driver's, manual wind, 14K yellow gold filled. *$1,500*
  *Watch courtesy of Charlie Cleves
  - Cleves and Lonnemann Jewelers*

(Right)

GRUEN

- Curvex, sub second, 14K pink gold filled, manual wind, 40mm. *$250 (in 14K pink gold, $550)*
  *Watch courtesy of Charlie Cleves
  - Cleves and Lonnemann Jewelers*

(Bottom Middle)

GRUEN

- Curvex, manual wind, 10K yellow gold filled, 40mm. *$250 (in 14K, $500)*
  *Watch courtesy of Charlie Cleves
  - Cleves and Lonnemann Jewelers*

(Bottom Right)

GRUEN

- Curvex Baron, manual wind, piecrust edge, 10K yellow gold filled, 43mm. *$400*
  *Watch courtesy of Charlie Cleves
  - Cleves and Lonnemann Jewelers*

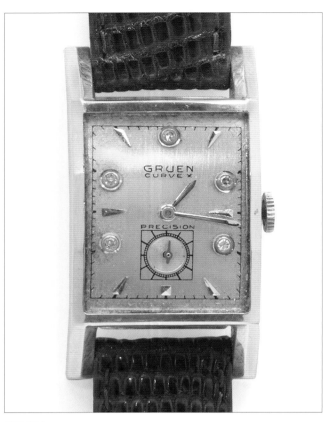

GRUEN
- Curvex, flared case in 10K gold filled, circa 1940s. *$350*

Watch courtesy of Tim and Reyne Haines

GRUEN
- Curvex, 14K yellow gold, sub second, manual wind. *$175*

Watch courtesy of Chris Miller

GRUEN
- Curvex, silver dial, diamond markers, 14K yellow gold, 40mm. *$700*

Watch courtesy of Charlie Cleves - Cleves and Lonnemann Jewelers

GRUEN
- Curvex, fancy lugs, manual wind, 14K yellow gold. *$400*

Watch courtesy of Charlie Cleves - Cleves and Lonnemann Jewelers

GRUEN
- Manual wind, black enamel Roman numerals, 14K yellow gold. *$350*

Watch courtesy of Charlie Cleves - Cleves and Lonnemann Jewelers

GRUEN
- Curvex, diamond bezel, diamond markers, manual wind, 14K white gold. *$500*

Watch courtesy of Charlie Cleves - Cleves and Lonnemann Jewelers

GRUEN
- Veri-Thin Precision, faceted crystal, manual wind, 10K yellow gold filled. *$150*

Watch courtesy of Charlie Cleves - Cleves and Lonnemann Jewelers

GRUEN
- Veri-Thin Precision, sub second, hinged lugs, manual wind, applied numerals. *$175*

Watch courtesy of Charlie Cleves - Cleves and Lonnemann Jewelers

GRUEN
- Curvex, circa 1940, case 44mm x 21mm, curved back, stepped bezel sides, gold-filled. *$350*

Watch courtesy of Heritage Auction Galleries

GRUEN
- Precision, enamel bezel, manual wind, 14K yellow gold. *$900*

Watch courtesy of Charlie Cleves - Cleves and Lonnemann Jewelers

GRUEN
- Driver's, manual wind, yellow gold filled. *$700*

Watch courtesy of Charlie Cleves - Cleves and Lonnemann Jewelers

GRUEN
- Curvex, driver's, manual wind, 14K yellow gold filled. *$900*

Watch courtesy of Charlie Cleves - Cleves and Lonnemann Jewelers

GRUEN
- Curvex, manual wind, 14K yellow gold filled, 43mm. *$400*

Watch courtesy of Charlie Cleves - Cleves and Lonnemann Jewelers

GRUEN
- Curvex circa 1930s, 14K yellow gold, curved back, stepped bezel, gold Arabic numerals, sub-seconds, manual wind. *$1,000*

Watch courtesy of Heritage Auction Galleries

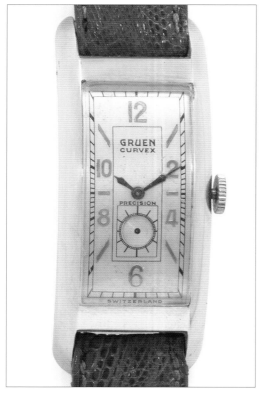

GRUEN
- Curvex Majesty, manual wind, 14K yellow gold filled, 52mm. *$2,000*

Watch courtesy of Charlie Cleves - Cleves and Lonnemann Jewelers

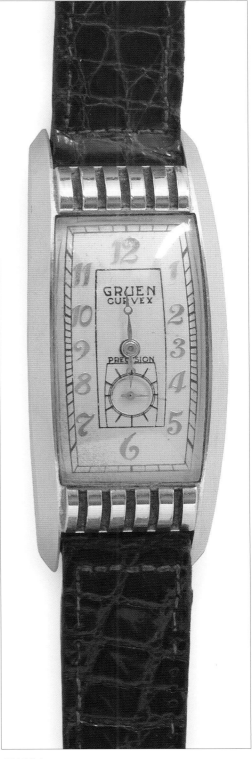

(Above)
GRUEN
• Manual wind, sub
  second, yellow gold
  filled and stainless steel
  back, 46mm. *$250*
  Watch courtesy of Charlie Cleves
  - Cleves and Lonnemann Jewelers

(Top Right)
GRUEN
• Curvex, manual wind, yellow
  gold filled, 48mm. *$600*
  Watch courtesy of Charlie Cleves
  - Cleves and Lonnemann Jewelers

(Right)
GRUEN
• Curvex, silver dial, applied
  gold numerals, manual
  wind, 14K yellow gold
  filled, 43mm. *$300*
  Watch courtesy of Charlie Cleves
  - Cleves and Lonnemann Jewelers

GRUEN
• Curvex Triumph, with ribs, manual wind,
  14K yellow gold filled, 51mm. *$2,000*
  Watch courtesy of Charlie Cleves - Cleves and Lonnemann Jewelers

GRUEN
- Curvex, manual wind, silver dial, applied gold numbers, 14K yellow gold, 52mm. *$7,500*

Watch courtesy of Charlie Cleves - Cleves and Lonnemann Jewelers

(Above)
GRUEN
- Curvex, black and gold dial, manual wind, 14K yellow gold filled, 41mm. *$250*

Watch courtesy of Charlie Cleves - Cleves and Lonnemann Jewelers

(Top Left)
GRUEN
- Curvex, black and gold dial, manual wind, 14K yellow gold filled, 41mm. *$250*

Watch courtesy of Charlie Cleves - Cleves and Lonnemann Jewelers

(Left)
GRUEN
- Long case, manual wind, yellow gold and stainless steel back, 46mm. *$200*

Watch courtesy of Charlie Cleves - Cleves and Lonnemann Jewelers

(Right)
GRUEN
- Curvex, manual wind, yellow gold filled and stainless steel back, 46mm.   *$200*

Watch courtesy of Charlie Cleves - Cleves and Lonnemann Jewelers

(Below)
GRUEN
- Curvex, manual wind, 14K yellow gold filled, long case, 45 mm.   *$400*

Watch courtesy of Charlie Cleves - Cleves and Lonnemann Jewelers

(Bottom Center)
GRUEN
- Curvex, gold dial with applied gold numerals, manual wind, 46mm.   *$400*

Watch courtesy of Charlie Cleves - Cleves and Lonnemann Jewelers

GRUEN
- Curvex, applied gold numerals, manual wind, 14K yellow gold, 48mm.   *$1,600*

Watch courtesy of Charlie Cleves - Cleves and Lonnemann Jewelers

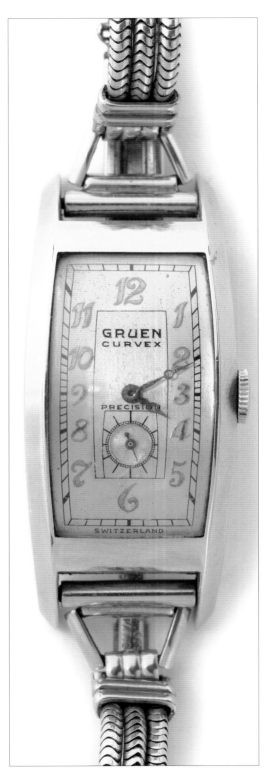

GRUEN
- Curvex Triumph, manual wind,
  yellow gold filled. *$1,200*

Watch courtesy of Charlie Cleves - Cleves and Lonnemann Jewelers

(Above)
GRUEN
- Lady's, 14K gold and
  diamonds, Arabic numeral
  indicators, bezel with single-
  cut diamonds, adjustable
  gold mesh strap. *$550*

Watch courtesy of Skinner Inc.

(Right)
GRUEN
- Lady's Veri-Thin, manual
  wind, nurse's, yellow
  gold filled, stainless
  steel back. *$75*

*Watch courtesy of Charlie Cleves
- Cleves and Lonnemann Jewelers*

(Bottom Right)
GRUEN
- Lady's, early manual wind,
  14K yellow gold. *$150*

*Watch courtesy of Charlie Cleves
- Cleves and Lonnemann Jewelers*

(Above)
GRUEN
• Lady's Curvex, manual wind, 10K
 yellow gold filled. *$85*
 Watch courtesy of Charlie Cleves - Cleves and Lonnemann Jewelers

(Left)
GRUEN
• Lady's Curvex, manual wind, 14K
 yellow gold filled, 47 mm. *$300*
 Watch courtesy of Charlie Cleves - Cleves and Lonnemann Jewelers

(Right)
GRUEN
• Lady's Precision, 14K white gold with
 diamonds, manual wind. *$300*
 Watch courtesy of Charlie Cleves - Cleves and Lonnemann Jewelers

(Above)
GRUEN
• Lady's Curvex, 10K pink gold
  filled, manual wind. *$100*
  Watch courtesy of Charlie Cleves - Cleves and Lonnemann Jewelers

(Right)
GRUEN
• Lady's Curvex, 10K pink gold
  filled, manual wind. *$125*
  Watch courtesy of Charlie Cleves - Cleves and Lonnemann Jewelers

(Far Right)
GRUEN
• Lady's, manual wind, engraved bezel,
  gold filled, sapphires. *$150*
  Watch courtesy of Charlie Cleves - Cleves and Lonnemann Jewelers

GÜBELIN

The watch shop of Gübelin opened in 1854 in Lucerne, Switzerland, originally owned by watchmaker Jakob Josef Mauritz Breitschmid. It wasn't until years later that the company became known as Gübelin. Breitschmid hired an apprentice, Eduard Jakob Gübelin, who eventually married Breitschmid's daughter, Bertha, and purchased the company in 1899.

Today, the company is still family owned.

(Above)
GÜBELIN
• 18K yellow gold, Patek Philippe movement, manual wind. *$4,250*
Watch courtesy of Leslie Hindman Auctioneers

(Left)
GÜBELIN
• Memovox Automatic Alarm, 1950s. Center seconds, self-winding, water-resistant, stainless steel with date, alarm and two crowns. *$4,000*
Image courtesy of Antiquorum Auctioneers

(Middle Right)
GÜBELIN
• Stainless steel, manual wind, luminescent numbers. *$100*
Watch courtesy of Phil Lucas

(Bottom Right)
GÜBELIN
• Stainless steel, manual wind, black dial, gold bar markers. *$125*
Watch courtesy of Phil Lucas

HAMILTON

ongtime American watch company Hamilton was founded in 1892 in Lancaster, Pa. They debuted their first watch in 1893. Known for their railroad pocket watches, Hamilton also produced a similar design as a wristwatch model. This watch would be worn by the American military, to the North and South Poles, and to the top of Mt. Everest.

After the Yankees won the World Series in 1928, Hamilton introduced the "Yankee" watch, along with the "Piping Rock." Both watches were cutting-edge designs for the time.

Soon after, Hamilton caught the eye of the airline industry. Their watches became the timepiece of choice for Eastern, Northwest, TWA and United Airlines.

During World War II, Hamilton stopped production of watches for the consumer to create watches for the military. It is estimated that one million Hamilton military watches are produced during that time.

Hamilton proved to be a leader in innovation again after creating the first electric watch in 1957. The "Ventura" was an instant success. Because of its sleek design, the Ventura found a fan in Elvis Presley, who wore the watch in the movie, "Blue Hawaii."

Hamilton is still in production today.

(Above)
HAMILTON
- Piping Rock, circa 1937, 14K yellow gold with hinged lugs, enameled bezel with Roman chapters. *$900*
Watch courtesy of Heritage Auction Galleriesv

(Far Left)
HAMILTON
- Piping Rock, circa 1937, 14K yellow gold, black enameled bezel with Roman numerals, hinged lugs, manual wind. *$1,000*
Watch courtesy of Heritage Auction Galleries

(Left)
HAMILTON
- Piping Rock, circa 1935, 14K white gold, snap back, hinged lugs, enameled bezel with Roman chapters, manual wind. *$1,000*
Watch courtesy of Heritage Auction Galleries

(Right Top)
HAMILTON
- Manual wind, silver dial, sub second, black numbers, 10K yellow gold filled. *$100*
Watch courtesy of Charlie Cleves - Cleves and Lonnemann Jewelers

(Right Middle)
HAMILTON
ELECTRIC
- Railroad Special, black numerals, 10K yellow gold filled. *$200*
Watch courtesy of Phil Lucas

(Below)
HAMILTON
- "gold eagle like" dial, 33.5mm, gold plated, 22 jewel. *$300*
Watch courtesy of Derek Dier, WatchesToBuy.com

HAMILTON
- Electric, Sea-Lectric, cal. 500, gold filled, 1958. *$795*
Watch courtesy of Derek Dier, WatchesToBuy.com

(Right)
HAMILTON

- Manual wind, sub
second, diamond
numerals, fancy
lugs, 14K yellow
gold. *$275*
Watch courtesy of Phil Lucas

(Far Right)
HAMILTON

- Electric, Polaris 2,
29mm, gold filled,
circa 1965. *$975*
*Watch courtesy of Derek
Dier, WatchesToBuy.com*

(Below)
HAMILTON

- 14K white gold
and diamonds,
manual wind, circa
1950. *$500*
*Watch courtesy of Heritage
Auction Galleries*

(Far Left)
HAMILTON

- Electric, custom
dial, 34mm, stainless
steel. *$595*
*Watch courtesy of Derek
Dier, WatchesToBuy.com*

(Left)
HAMILTON

- Odyssey 2001,
38mm, stainless steel,
automatic. *$700*
*Watch courtesy of Derek
Dier, WatchesToBuy.com*

(Top Left)
HAMILTON ELECTRIC
• "Spectra 2," circa 1963, scarce. *$1,500*
  Watch courtesy of Derek Dier, WatchesToBuy.com

(Top Middle)
HAMILTON ELECTRIC
• In stainless steel. *$150*
  Watch courtesy of Leslie Hindman Auctioneers

(Top Right)
HAMILTON ELECTRIC
• 10K yellow gold filled. *$150*
  Watch courtesy of Leslie Hindman Auctioneers

(Bottom Far Left)
HAMILTON
• Electric, Polaris, stainless steel. *$250*
  Watch courtesy of Phil Lucas

(Bottom Left)
HAMILTON ELECTRIC
• 10K yellow gold filled. *$225*
  Watch courtesy of Phil Lucas

(Right)
HAMILTON
- Electric, Everest in 10K gold filled, circa 1960s.   *$525*
  Watch courtesy of Tim and Reyne Haines

(Far Right)
HAMILTON
- Manual wind, silver dial, gold applied numerals, 10K rose gold plated bezel.   *$100*
  Watch courtesy of Tim and Reyne Haines

(Below)
HAMILTON
- Electric, Everest, 10K yellow gold filled.   *$250*
  Watch courtesy of Phil Lucas

HAMILTON
- Electric, Everest, gold filled, cal. 500, 29mm, circa 1958.   *$900*
  Watch courtesy of Derek Dier, WatchesToBuy.com

(Left)
HAMILTON
- Pacer, automatic, circa 1960, yellow gold-filled body, white gold-filled lugs, No. S 528502. *$1,500*
Watch courtesy of Heritage Auction Galleries

(Top Right)
HAMILTON
- Electric, Pacer in 10K gold filled, circa 1960s. *$700*
Watch courtesy of Tim and Reyne Haines

(Right)
HAMILTON
- Pacer, gold filled, yellow center, white lugs, back inscribed, circa 1958. *$500*
Watch courtesy of Heritage Auction Galleries

HAMILTON
- Electric, Savitar, 14K gold, circa 1961. *$1,000*
Watch courtesy of Derek Dier, WatchesToBuy.com

HAMILTON
- Electric, Savitar, 10K yellow gold filled. *$250*
Watch courtesy of Phil Lucas

HAMILTON
- Electric, Pacer, gold filled two-tone, 31mm. *$850*
Watch courtesy of Derek Dier, WatchesToBuy.com

HAMILTON
- Electric, Savitar, 14K gold, circa 1961. *$900*
Watch courtesy of Derek Dier, WatchesToBuy.com

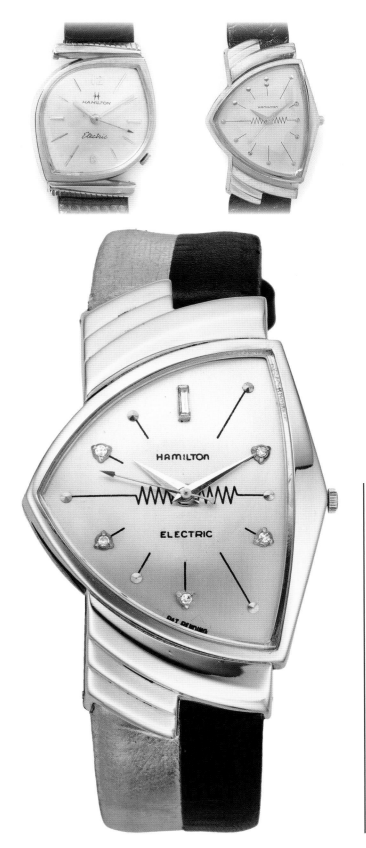

(Above)
HAMILTON
• Electric, Ventura, cal. 500, 14K gold, 1957.   *$2,500*
  Watch courtesy of Derek Dier, WatchesToBuy.com

(Top Left)
HAMILTON
• Electric, Victor II in 10K gold filled, circa 1960s.   *$425*
  Watch courtesy of Tim and Reyne Haines

(Top Middle)
HAMILTON
• Ventura, re-issue, circa 1990, 10K yellow gold.   *$345*
  Watch courtesy of Phil Lucas

(Left)
HAMILTON
• Ventura, circa 1957, 14K yellow gold, hooded stepped lugs, diamond and gold markers, electric, with custom box and history pamphlet.   *$2,500*
  Watch courtesy of Heritage Auction Galleries

HAMILTON

• Turner, manual wind, enamel numbers, 10K pink gold filled. *$200*

Watch courtesy of Charlie Cleves - Cleves and Lonnemann Jewelers

HAMILTON

• Watson, manual wind, applied gold numerals, sub second, 14K yellow gold filled. *$175*

Watch courtesy of Charlie Cleves - Cleves and Lonnemann Jewelers

HAMILTON

• Perry, manual wind, silver dial, pink gold applied numbers, circa 1930s. *$160*

Watch courtesy of Charlie Cleves - Cleves and Lonnemann Jewelers

(Top Left)

HAMILTON

- Yellow gold filled, manual wind, sub second, circa 1930s. *$75*

  Watch courtesy of Chris Miller

(Top Middle)

HAMILTON

- Rectangular, black enameled numerals, sub second, manual wind, 14K yellow gold filled. *$75*

  Watch courtesy of Phil Lucas

(Top Right)

HAMILTON

- Doctor's, 14K yellow gold filled, 1930s, manual wind. *$750*

  Watch courtesy of Chris Miller

(Right)

HAMILTON

- Dodson, manual wind, silver dial, applied gold numbers, sub second 10K yellow gold filled. *$175*

  Watch courtesy of Charlie Cleves - Cleves and Lonnemann Jewelers

(Far Right)

HAMILTON

- Manual wind, silver dial, luminescent markers, gold filled. *$200*

  Watch courtesy of Charlie Cleves - Cleves and Lonnemann Jewelers

HAMILTON
- Circa 1960s, 14K white gold, white gold batons, manual wind. *$500*

Watch courtesy of Heritage Auction Galleries

(Above)
HAMILTON
- Platinum with diamond dial, circa 1940s, platinum, sub seconds, diamond-set platinum markers and numerals. *$1,850*
Watch courtesy of Heritage Auction Galleries

(Top Left)
HAMILTON
- Diamond rectangle, 14K white gold, circa 1940, manual wind. *$950*
Watch courtesy of Chris Miller

(Left)
HAMILTON
- Circa 1940s, diamond bezel, diamond markers and numerals, sub seconds, manual wind, 14K white gold band. *$2,200*
Watch courtesy of Heritage Auction Galleries

HAMILTON
- Platinum, diamond dial, curved back, unique circular lugs, circa 1940s. *$3,150*
Watch courtesy of Heritage Auction Galleries

(Left)
HAMILTON

- Lady's, manual wind, platinum with diamonds. *$4,500*

  Watch courtesy of Charlie Cleves - Cleves and Lonnemann Jewelers

(Right)
HAMILTON

- Lady's, manual wind, 14K white gold with diamonds. *$950*

  Watch courtesy of Charlie Cleves - Cleves and Lonnemann Jewelers

(Below)
HAMILTON

- Platinum and diamonds, manual wind, circa 1950. *$1,500*

  Watch courtesy of Leslie Hindman Auctioneers

(Left)

HAMILTON

- Lady's, circa 1940, 14K yellow gold, hinged lugs, rope band, manual wind.   *$100*

  Watch courtesy of Heritage Auction Galleries

(Right)

HAMILTON

- Lady's, circa 1940s, platinum, set with diamonds, applied Arabic numerals, manual wind.   *$2,000*

  Watch courtesy of Heritage Auction Galleries

(Below)

HAMILTON

- Lady's, manual wind, 14K white gold with diamonds.   *$850*

  Watch courtesy of Charlie Cleves - Cleves and Lonnemann Jewelers

(Right)

HAMILTON

- Lady's, manual wind, 14K white gold with diamonds. *$1,200*

  Watch courtesy of Charlie Cleves - Cleves and Lonnemann Jewelers

(Far Top Right)

HAMILTON

- 14K white gold and diamonds, manual wind. *$900*

  Watch courtesy of Heritage Auction Galleries

(Bottom Right)

HAMILTON

- Lady's, manual wind, 14K white gold with diamonds. *$700*

  Watch courtesy of Charlie Cleves - Cleves and Lonnemann Jewelers

(Below)

HAMILTON

- Lady's, circa 1940s, 14K white gold, diamond-set bezel and lugs. *$350*

  Watch courtesy of Heritage Auction Galleries

(Far Left)
HAMILTON

- Lady's, manual wind, oval dial, 14K white gold with diamonds. *$1,200*

  Watch courtesy of Charlie Cleves - Cleves and Lonnemann Jewelers

(Top Middle)
HAMILTON

- Lady's, circa 1950, 14K white gold, diamonds, 34 x 15 mm, manual wind. *$175*

  Watch courtesy of Heritage Auction Galleries

(Bottom Middle)
HAMILTON

- Lady's, manual wind, pear-shaped dial, 14K white gold with diamonds. *$850*

  Watch courtesy of Charlie Cleves - Cleves and Lonnemann Jewelers

(Left)
HAMILTON

- Lady's, manual wind, 14K white gold with diamonds. *$400*

  Watch courtesy of Charlie Cleves - Cleves and Lonnemann Jewelers

(Below)
HAMILTON

- Lady's, manual wind, 14K white gold with diamonds. *$800*

  Watch courtesy of Charlie Cleves - Cleves and Lonnemann Jewelers

(Second from Left)

HAMILTON

- Lady's, circa 1940s, platinum, full diamond bezel and band, applied Arabic numerals. *$1,000*

  Watch courtesy of Heritage Auction Galleries

(Left)

HAMILTON

- 14K white gold and diamonds, manual wind. *$850*

  Watch courtesy of Heritage Auction Galleries

(Above)

HAMILTON

- 14K white gold and diamonds. *$800*

  Watch courtesy of Leslie Hindman Auctioneers

(Right)

HAMILTON

- Lady's, manual wind, platinum with diamonds. *$1,200*

  Watch courtesy of Charlie Cleves - Cleves and Lonnemann Jewelers

(Far Left)

LADY HAMILTON

- Manual wind, platinum with diamonds. *$2,000*

  Watch courtesy of Charlie Cleves - Cleves and Lonnemann Jewelers

(Above)

HAMILTON

- 14K white gold and diamonds, manual wind, circa 1930s. *$1,200*

Watch courtesy of Leslie Hindman Auctioneers

(Far Left)

HAMILTON

- Lady's, manual wind, 14K white gold with diamonds. *$750*

Watch courtesy of Charlie Cleves - Cleves and Lonnemann Jewelers

(Left)

HAMILTON

- Lady's, manual wind, 14K white gold and diamonds. *$400*

Watch courtesy of Charlie Cleves - Cleves and Lonnemann Jewelers

(Right)

HAMILTON

- Platinum and diamonds, manual wind, 10K white gold bracelet, circa 1950. *$775*

Watch courtesy of Heritage Auction Galleries

(Below)

HAMILTON

- Lady's, platinum and diamonds, manual wind. *$350*

Watch courtesy of Leslie Hindman Auctioneers

HELBROS

*H*elbros watches made their debut in 1913. The name "Helbros" was short for the founding Helbein Brothers. The Helbeins were Swiss-German watchmakers who decided to challenge the watch market, and instead of creating watches for the affluent, they decided to make them affordable to the masses.

In the 1960s, they designed a watch that told lunar time. Today, Helbros is still producing fine quality, affordable timepieces.

HELBROS
- Chronograph, Valjoux 7733 manual wind, 37.5mm, stainless steel. *$795*

Watch courtesy of Derek Dier, WatchesToBuy.com

HEUER

*H*euer was founded in St. Imier, Switzerland, by Edouard Heuer in 1860.

In 1882, Heuer patented its first chronograph, a style of watch they would be famous for. In 1911 the firm introduced the first dashboard chronograph for automobiles. By 1933, Heuer was producing dashboard watches for racecars. In 1975 they would produce the world's first quartz chronograph, and from 1971 to 1979, they were the official timekeeper for Formula One racing.

Heuer watches are known for their accuracy. They invented a stopwatch in 1916 that is accurate within 1/100th of a second. The Paris and Amsterdam Olympics chose Heuer as their official timekeeper.

In 1985, Heuer joined the TAG group, and the company name became Tag-Heuer.

HEUER
- Yacht Timer, Ref. 653.515, circa 1970. Unusual, large, composite waterproof wrist counter designed for boat races, with central 5-minute register. *$750*

Image courtesy of Antiquorum Auctioneers

HEUER
- Flieger, pilot's chronograph, 39mm, manual wind, rare, circa 1940. *$10,000*

Watch courtesy of Derek Dier, WatchesToBuy.com

HEUER
- Bund, 43mm, stainless steel, Valjoux manual wind. *$2,950*

Watch courtesy of Derek Dier, WatchesToBuy.com

(Above)
HEUER
• Autavia, "Jo Siffert," 17 jewel automatic, 43mm, stainless steel.   *$4,500*
  Watch courtesy of Derek Dier, WatchesToBuy.co

(Top Middle)
HEUER
• Autavia chronograph, two-register date, left-hand wind, 1970s.   *$1,500*
  Watch courtesy of Tim and Reyne Haines

(Top Right)
HEUER
• Autavia, stainless steel, automatic, chronograph.   *$2,200*
  Watch courtesy of Leslie Hindman Auctioneers

(Right)
HEUER
• Monaco, 40mm, stainless steel, Valjoux 7740 movement.   *$5,000*
  Watch courtesy of Derek Dier, WatchesToBuy.com

ILLINOIS

*T*he Illinois Springfield Watch Co. was founded in 1870. It had an unusual array of founders — John C. Adams, George Black, John W. Bunn, William B. Miller, George Passfield and John T. Stuart — none of them watchmakers.

Stuart was a lawyer and former partner of Abraham Lincoln. Miller was a local merchant. Williams was a bank president, and Bunn and his brother owned a grocery business. This did not stop the company from being profitable.

Their first pocket watch was produced in 1872 and was called the "Stuart." Illinois was well known for their railroad pocket watches.

Over the years, the company name changed from the Illinois Springfield Watch Co. to the Springfield Illinois Watch Co., then later to the Illinois Watch Co. The company was purchased by Hamilton in the 1920s. They continued to produce Illinois watches until 1932.

(Above)
ILLINOIS
- New Yorker, manual wind, stainless steel, sub second at 6. *$350*

  Watch courtesy of Phil Lucas

(Left)
ILLINOIS
- Guardsman, secometer dial, manual wind, luminescent numbers. *$750*

  Watch courtesy of Charlie Cleves - Cleves and Lonnemann Jewelers

(Below)
ILLINOIS
- Manual wind, sub second, gold numerals, yellow gold-filled shell. *$50*

  Watch courtesy of Phil Lucas

(Above)
ILLINOIS

- Marquis, manual wind,
  sub second at 9,
  stainless steel. *$225*
  Watch courtesy of Charlie Cleves
  - Cleves and Lonnemann Jewelers

(Left)
ILLINOIS

- Stainless steel with
  engraved case, circa
  1930. *$175*
  Watch courtesy of Tim
  and Reyne Haines

(Right)
ILLINOIS

- Lady's, Edgewaters,
  14K white gold filled,
  manual wind. *$75*
  Watch courtesy of Charlie Cleves
  - Cleves and Lonnemann Jewelers

(Far Right)
ILLINOIS

- "Off Duty," manual wind,
  black enamel numerals,
  sub second. *$1,000*
  Watch courtesy of Phil Lucas

(Top Left)
ILLINOIS
- Larchmont, manual wind, sub second, silver dial, gold numbers, yellow gold filled.   *$250*
Watch courtesy of Charlie Cleves - Cleves and Lonnemann Jewelers

(Middle Left)
ILLINOIS
- Step dial, manual wind, 10K gold filled.   *$50*
Watch courtesy of Phil Lucas

(Right(
ILLINOIS
- Lady's Art Deco, enamel, manual wind, gold filled.   *$200*
Watch courtesy of Charlie Cleves - Cleves and Lonnemann Jewelers

(Bottom Right)
ILLINOIS
- Hawthorne, manual wind, silver dial, gold numerals, sub second, stainless steel.   *$200*
Watch courtesy of Charlie Cleves - Cleves and Lonnemann Jewelers

(Bottom Left)
ILLINOIS
- Futura, manual wind, silver dial, sub second, yellow gold filled.   *$400*
Watch courtesy of Charlie Cleves - Cleves and Lonnemann Jewelers

ILLINOIS

- Guardian, manual wind, silver dial, black enamel numbers. *$200*

ILLINOIS

- Atlantic, manual wind, luminescent numbers, sub second, stainless steel. *$200*

(Left)
ILLINOIS

- Lady's, Berkeley, enamel Art Deco case, manual wind, circa 1930s, gold filled. *$125*

(Below)
ILLINOIS

- Ritz, manual wind, silver dial, black enamel numbers, gold filled and stainless steel back. *$700*

ILLINOIS

- Cushion Master, luminescent numbers, manual wind, sub second at 9. *$150*

ILLINOIS

- Blackstone, manual wind, black dial, orange hands and numbers, yellow gold filled. *$250*

ILLINOIS

- Ace, manual wind, luminescent numbers, sub second, yellow gold filled. *$200*

ILLINOIS

- Beau Brummell, sterling silver, manual wind, sub second, yellow gold filled. *$350*

IWC (INTERNATIONAL WATCH COMPANY)

*I*nternational Watch Company (IWC) opened in 1868 in Schaffhausen, Switzerland. It was founded by an American watchmaker, Florentine Ariosto Jones.

Jones had worked in the American watch industry for several years. He acquired a failed watch company in America, originally owned by Aaron Lufkin Dennison, and moved it to Switzerland. Without proper financing, and the high tariff in America on imported finished watches, he later filed for bankruptcy.

The company was purchased by a Swiss consortium, and another American was put in his place. Unfortunately, things did not go well with the new management and the business was put up for auction. It was purchased by one of the stockholders, and after a few advances in the pocket-watch market, put the company back on track.

As with many watchmakers, World War II created a need for large production of watches. IWC at this time created the first oversize, anti-magnetic pilot's watch. After the war ended, IWC would go on to create specialty watches such as the "Mark XI," and also the "Ingenieur."

Today, IWC is the manufacturer of the Porsche sports watch series. They are also known for creating the most complicated watch in the world, the "Il Destriero Scafusia."

(Far Left)
INTERNATIONAL WATCH CO.
• Circa 1950s, 18K yellow gold, long curved lugs, gold Arabic numerals.   *$1,000*
Watch courtesy of Heritage Auction Galleries

(Top Left)
INTERNATIONAL WATCH CO.
• Circa 1920, 14K gold, Arabic numerals, dial signed "International Watch Co."   *$700*
Watch courtesy of Heritage Auction Galleries

(Bottom Right)
INTERNATIONAL WATCH CO.
• Large center seconds, circa 1960s, 18K yellow gold, long curved teardrop lugs, 37 mm, manual wind.   *$800*
Watch courtesy of Heritage Auction Galleries

(Above)
INTERNATIONAL WATCH CO.
- Vintage fancy lugs, circa 1950, 14K yellow gold, applied numerals, manual wind. *$750*
  Watch courtesy of Heritage Auction Galleries

(Top Right)
INTERNATIONAL WATCH CO.
- Schaffhausen, 18K gold, Arabic and abstract numeral indicators, manual wind, 14K woven gold bracelet. *$1,500*
  Watch courtesy of Skinner Inc.

(Below)
INTERNATIONAL WATCH CO.
- 18K yellow gold, sweep second hand. *$1,000*
  Watch courtesy of Heritage Auction Galleries

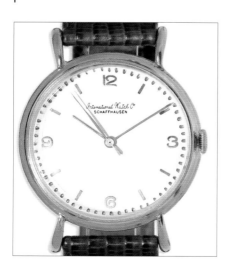

INTERNATIONAL WATCH CO.
- 33mm, 18K rose gold, manual wind, 1950s. *$2,450*
  Watch courtesy of Derek Dier, WatchesToBuy.com

INTERNATIONAL WATCH CO.
- Schaffhausen, movement No. 1250445, case No. 1248836, 1960s, 18K yellow gold. *$1,250*

  Image courtesy of Antiquorum Auctioneers

INTERNATIONAL WATCH CO.
- Steel, circa 1950, snap back, long curved lugs, raised gold markers, manual wind. *$450*

  Watch courtesy of Heritage Auction Galleries

INTERNATIONAL WATCH CO.
- Schaffhausen, automatic, No. 1229408, late 1950s. Center seconds, self-winding, 18K yellow gold. *$2,500*

  Image courtesy of Antiquorum Auctioneers

JAEGER-LECOULTRE

Antoine LeCoultre

*L*eCoultre & Cie was founded in 1833 by Antoine LeCoultre. LeCoultre was known for being an inventor and his devotion to precision wristwatch design. As early as 1844, he was measuring microns and developed the world's most precise measuring instrument, the "Millionometer," which measured components to the nearest thousandth of a millimeter.

The quality of movements LeCoultre designed did not go unnoticed. They were the main supplier for movements for the Patek Philippe until 1910.

LeCoultre's motto was: "We must base our experience on science." The firm became the leading supplier of movements, parts and tools to the watch-making industry in Switzerland. From 1910-1919, LeCoultre produced approximately 40,000 movements. They were sold for 100 to 400 French francs each.

In 1925, the grandson of the founder, Jacques-David LeCoultre, met Parisian watchmaker Edmond Jaeger. At the time, Jaeger was the exclusive supplier of watch movements for Cartier. From their friendship, a new venture was born: Jaeger-LeCoultre.

A few of the most recognizable watches made by Jaeger-LeCoultre are the "Reverso," the "Futurematic" and the "Memovox." In the 1960s, an Italian dealer came to visit the factory. He bought several Reverso cases, fitted them with movements, and took them back for sale. The watches sold out immediately. Today, the Reverso is the most popular model made.

Jaeger-LeCoultre is still in business today. Their factory is only a few feet away from the site of where the original factory stood. To date, they still manufacture their own bracelets, cases, dials, hands and movements.

(Far Left)
JAEGER-LECOULTRE
- **$20 gold coin, 18K yellow gold, manual wind.** *$2,750*

  Watch courtesy of Heritage Auction Galleries

(Left)
JAEGER-LECOULTRE
- **Alarm, 38.5mm, stainless steel, automatic, 1974.** *$2,450*

  Watch courtesy of Derek Dier, WatchesToBuy.com

LECOULTRE
- 14K yellow gold, manual wind, circa 1970s. *$650*
  Watch courtesy of Leslie Hindman Auctioneers

JAEGER-LECOULTRE
- Stainless steel, automatic. *$475*
  Watch courtesy of Leslie Hindman Auctioneers

(Top Left)
JAEGER-LECOULTRE
- Polaris, alarm, 42mm, stainless steel automatic, circa 1968 (rare). *$15,000*
  Watch courtesy of Derek Dier, WatchesToBuy.com

(Top Right)
JAEGER-LECOULTRE
- 18K gold, 35mm, manual wind with teardrop lugs. *$2,500*
  Watch courtesy of Derek Dier, WatchesToBuy.com

(Bottom Far Left)
JAEGER-LECOULTRE
- Alarm, circa 1955, flared lugs, yellow gold-filled, two-body, double winding crowns. *$650*
  Watch courtesy of Heritage Auction Galleries

(Middle Left)
JAEGER-LECOULTRE
- Stainless steel, automatic, circa 1950s, Calatrava-type lugs, 34 mm, triple signed Jaeger-LeCoultre. *$550*
  Watch courtesy of Heritage Auction Galleries

(Middle Bottom)
LECOULTRE
- Automatic, inscribed on back, 10K gold filled, circa 1955. *$175*
  Watch courtesy of Phil Lucas

(Top Left)
JAEGER-LECOULTRE
• Memovox, No. 729735, case No. 533215, late 1950s. Center seconds, 18K yellow gold with alarm and two crowns. *$1,500*
Image courtesy of Antiquorum Auctioneers

(Top Middle)
JAEGER-LECOULTRE
• Memovox, No. 760780, case No. 547302, 1950s. Center seconds, 18K yellow gold with alarm and two crowns. *$2,000*
Image courtesy of Antiquorum Auctioneers

(Bottom Left)
JAEGER-LECOULTRE
• "Master Control," stainless steel. *$3,500*
Watch courtesy of Heritage Auction Galleries

(Bottom Middle)
LECOULTRE
• Automatic, power reserve indicator, 10K yellow gold filled. *$650*
Watch courtesy of Phil Lucas

(Bottom Right)
LECOULTRE
• Lady's, manual wind, fancy lugs, 14K yellow gold filled. *$175*
Watch courtesy of Tim and Reyne Haines

(Left)
JAEGER-LECOULTRE
- Stainless steel, manual wind. *$150*

Watch courtesy of Leslie Hindman Auctioneers

(Right)
JAEGER-LECOULTRE
- Club, circa 1960, screw back, stainless steel, 34 mm. *$1,195*

Watch courtesy of Heritage Auction Galleries

(Bottom Right)
LECOULTRE
- Memovox, alarm, 10K gold filled, automatic, circa 1950s. *$400*

Watch courtesy of Chris Miller

(Below)
JAEGER-LECOULTRE
- Master Mariner, circa 1960s, stainless steel, 35 mm, heavy lugs. *$650*

Watch courtesy of Heritage Auction Galleries

LECOULTRE

• Futurematic, circa 1951. Self-
  winding, 10K yellow gold-
  filled with 40-hour power
  reserve indicator.   *$1,200*

Image courtesy of Antiquorum Auctioneers

LECOULTRE

• Futurematic, yellow
  gold filled.   *$950*

Watch courtesy of Phil Lucas

LECOULTRE

• Futurematic, 35mm, cal. 497 automatic, gold filled.   *$1,250*

Watch courtesy of Derek Dier, WatchesToBuy.com

LECOULTRE
- Futurematic, gold filled, 35mm, 17 jewel automatic, 1950s   *$1,450*

Watch courtesy of Derek Dier, WatchesToBuy.com

JAEGER-LECOULTRE
- No. 352448, case No. 328196, 1950s, 18K pink gold with triple date calendar.   *$2,500*

Image courtesy of Antiquorum Auctioneers

LECOULTRE
- New/old stock, circa 1950, gold-filled top, stainless steel back, #3421562, recessed crown, curved lugs.   *$400*

Watch courtesy of Heritage Auction Galleries

LECOULTRE
- Circa 1940s, 14K yellow gold, extended hooded lugs, curved crystal. *$1,075*

Watch courtesy of Heritage Auction Galleries

JAEGER-LECOULTRE
- Circa 1970s, 18K yellow gold, heavy two-piece, sapphire cabochon crown, manual wind. *$600*

Watch courtesy of Heritage Auction Galleries

LECOULTRE
- White gold filled, 23mm, 17 jewel manual wind, 1950s. *$1,150*

Watch courtesy of Derek Dier, WatchesToBuy.com

LECOULTRE
- Hooded lugs, manual wind, sub second, applied gold markers, NYFD dedication, 14K yellow gold. *$1,200*

Watch courtesy of Charlie Cleves - Cleves and Lonnemann Jewelers

LECOULTRE
- Manual wind, 14K yellow gold with diamond bezel, circa 1970s. *$800*

Watch courtesy of Chris Miller

(Below from Left to Right)
JAEGER-LECOULTRE
- Lady's. integral bracelet, circa 1970s, 18K white gold, 23 mm oval with brushed finish. *$500*

Watch courtesy of Heritage Auction Galleries

JAEGER-LECOULTRE
- Lady's, circa 1950, extra large claw lugs, 9K yellow gold, No. 2485. *$350*

Watch courtesy of Heritage Auction Galleries

LECOULTRE
- 14K yellow gold, lady's, manual wind, circa 1950s. *$775*

Watch courtesy of Leslie Hindman Auctioneers

JAEGER-LECOULTRE
- Day/Night Duoface Reverso, circa 1990, stainless steel, No. 1963020, model 270.8.54, rotating head, ribbed bezels. *$3,100*

Watch courtesy of Heritage Auction Galleries

(Above)
JAEGER-LECOULTRE
- Lady's, 18K yellow gold.   *$3,000*

Watch courtesy of Leslie Hindman Auctioneers

(Right)
LECOULTRE
- 14K white gold and diamonds.   *$200*

Watch courtesy of Leslie Hindman Auctioneers

(Far Right)
JAEGER-LECOULTRE
- 18K yellow gold, manual wind.   *$1,900*

Watch courtesy of Leslie Hindman Auctioneers

(Above)
LECOULTRE
- For Mauboussin, 18K yellow gold.   *$675*

Watch courtesy of Leslie Hindman Auctioneers

(Left)
LECOULTRE
- Lady's, fancy lugs, manual wind, 14K yellow gold.   *$400*

Watch courtesy of Charlie Cleves
- Cleves and Lonnemann Jewelers

JULES JURGENSEN

*P*ossibly one of the oldest watch-making companies in the world today, it was founded in 1740 by Jürgen Jürgensen under the original name of Larpent & Jürgensen.

It was in 1838 that Jürgensen's grandson, Jules, took over the company and began producing watches under the name "Jules Jürgensen." Production under this name lasted until 1957. Since then, production has been outsourced to other firms. Today, the company is owned by Mort Clayman, a watch distributor in the United States.

JULES JERGENSEN
- 14K yellow gold and diamonds, manual wind. $650

Watch courtesy of Leslie Hindman Auctioneers

JUVENIA

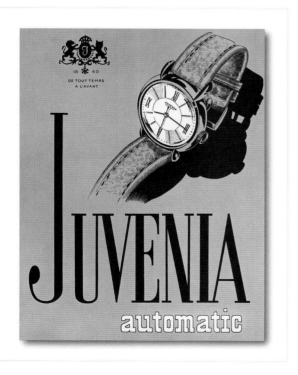

*I*n 1860, Jacques Didisheim founded the watch-making firm Juvenia in the town of La Chaux-de-Fonds. Juvenia is known for several firsts in the watch world. They created some of the first movements with lever escapement, and also the smallest movement measuring 2.5 millimeters thick and 9.5 millimeters wide.

JUVENIA
- Hooded lugs, case No. 93420, circa 1960. Center-seconds, 18K yellow gold. $1,250

Image courtesy of Antiquorum Auctioneers

JUVENIA
- Manual wind, agate dial, sapphire crystal, 18K yellow gold, circa 1960s. $1,800

Watch courtesy of Tim and Reyne Haines

LONGINES

*F*ounded in 1832 by Auguste Agassiz, in St. Imier, Switzerland, this was primarily an "assembler" of watches. Many of the company's craftsmen worked out of their homes.

For almost 20 years this method of business worked well and was quite profitable. In 1854, Agassiz was in poor health. He handed the business responsibilities to his nephew, Ernest Francillon, who built a factory nearby in the town of Les Longines and re-branded the line under the Longines name.

The company was best known for their chronographs and aviator watches. In the 1950s, Longines purchased another watch company, Wittnauer. The company continued to market both brand names in the United States.

LONGINES
- Lindbergh, hour angle, rotating bezel, yellow gold filled.   *$2,750*

Watch courtesy of Phil Lucas

(Above)
LONGINES
- 13ZN chronograph, No. 6057903, case No. 21153, Ref. 205, 1950s. Stainless steel with round-button chronograph, register, telemeter and tachometer.   *$12,500*

Image courtesy of Antiquorum Auctioneers

(Right)
LONGINES
- Lindbergh - Hour Angle, No. 5990960, case No. 9143058, replica of the navigator's watch invented by Charles Lindbergh and Longines, made 1950s to commemorate Lindbergh's first flight over the Atlantic Ocean in 1927. Hour-angle, center seconds, 10K yellow gold-filled. Accompanied by the original fitted box.   *$2,500*

Image courtesy of Antiquorum Auctioneers

LONGINES
- Circa 1950, 14K yellow gold, long
  tapered lugs, Arabic numerals,
  center sweep, automatic.   *$300*

  Watch courtesy of Heritage Auction Galleries

LONGINES
- Early steel, oversized, circa 1940, curved Calatrava-
  type lugs, Ref. 96, No. 22804.   *$950*

  Watch courtesy of Heritage Auction Galleries

LONGINES
- Manual wind, silver dial, gold markers,
  sub second, 14K yellow gold.   *$400*

  Watch courtesy of Charlie Cleves - Cleves and Lonnemann Jewelers

(Right)/
LONGINES

- Conquest, power reserve, 35mm, stainless steel, 24 jewel automatic, circa 1960s. *$1,750*

Watch courtesy of Derek Dier, WatchesToBuy.com

(Below)
LONGINES

- Weems, manual wind, center sweep, 14K yellow gold. *$700*

Watch courtesy of Charlie Cleves - Cleves and Lonnemann Jewelers

(Above)
LONGINES

- 10K yellow gold filled, manual wind. *$500*

Watch courtesy of Leslie Hindman Auctioneers

(Left)
LONGINES

- Comet, stainless steel, manual wind, circa 1970. *$1,250*

Watch courtesy of Phil Lucas

LONGINES
• "Mystérieuse," cased by Longines-Wittnauer Watch Co., New York-Montreal, No. 11250150, Ref. 1012, 1950s, 14K yellow gold. *$1,200*

Image courtesy of Antiquorum Auctioneers

LONGINES
• 18K yellow gold with a gold-plated Longines buckle, No. 12586439, Ref. 6900, 1960s, accompanied by a box. *$750*

Image courtesy of Antiquorum Auctioneers

LONGINES
• Art Deco, circa 1945, 14K yellow gold, black enamel hour marks on the bezel. *$700*

Watch courtesy of Heritage Auction Galleries

(Above)
LONGINES
• "Mystérieuse," 14K gold, 32.5mm, 17 jewel manual wind, 1960s. *$900*

Watch courtesy of Derek Dier, WatchesToBuy.com

(Top Right)
LONGINES
• Circa 1960s, 14K yellow gold, gold Arabic numerals, manual wind. *$200*

Watch courtesy of Heritage Auction Galleries

(Middle Right)
LONGINES
• Automatic, black dial, day, diamond marker, stainless steel. *$150*

Watch courtesy of Charlie Cleves - Cleves and Lonnemann Jewelers

(Bottom Right)
LONGINES
• "Mystérieuse," yellow gold filled. *$75*

Watch courtesy of Phil Lucas

(Left)

LONGINES

- 14K yellow gold, manual wind.   *$800*

  Watch courtesy of Leslie Hindman Auctioneers

(Top Middle)

LONGINES

- Fancy lugs, diamond dial, circa 1955, 14K white gold, manual wind, large scroll-form lugs.   *$1,350*

  Watch courtesy of Heritage Auction Galleries

(Top Right)

LONGINES

- "Mystérieuse," cased by Longines-Wittnauer Watch Co., New York-Montreal, No. 11249751, Ref. 1017, 1950s, 14K white gold and diamonds.   *$1,500*

  Image courtesy of Antiquorum Auctioneers

(Above)

LONGINES

- Yellow gold filled, manual wind, sub second.   *$150*

  Watch courtesy of Leslie Hindman Auctioneers

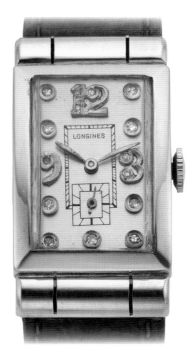

LONGINES
• Diamond dial, circa 1940s, 14K gold, curved back, large hooded barrel-form lugs. $1,200
Watch courtesy of Heritage Auction Galleries

(Left)
LONGINES
• Manual wind, diamond markers, 14K white gold. $350
Watch courtesy of Charlie Cleves - Cleves and Lonnemann Jewelers

(Right)
LONGINES
• Manual wind, diamond markers, 14K white gold. $600
Watch courtesy of Charlie Cleves - Cleves and Lonnemann Jewelers

(Below)
LONGINES
• 14K white gold and diamonds, midsize, modern. $1,200
Watch courtesy of Heritage Auction Galleries

LONGINES
• Advocate, black dial, manual wind, diamond markers, 14K white gold. $1,200
Watch courtesy of Charlie Cleves - Cleves and Lonnemann Jewelers

(Right)
AGASSIZ
- 18K yellow gold, sub second, dial signed Tiffany & Co, manual wind, circa 1926. *$1,500*
  Watch courtesy of Heritage Auction Galleries

(Far Right)
LONGINES
- Lady's, rectangle, black enamel, manual wind, stainless steel. *$75*
  Watch courtesy of Phil Lucas

(Below)
LONGINES
- Circa 1940, 14K yellow gold, sub seconds, gold batons, gold numerals and bar markers, manual wind. *$350*
  Watch courtesy of Heritage Auction Galleries

(Above)
LONGINES
• Lady's, No. 9998652, case No. 423257, Ref. 601, late 1950s. Square, 14K yellow gold with a double leather cord bracelet. *$500*
Image courtesy of Antiquorum Auctioneers

(Left)
LONGINES
• Platinum with diamonds, platinum bracelet, circa 1948. *$700*
Watch courtesy of Heritage Auction Galleries

(Right)
LONGINES
• 14K white gold and diamonds, manual wind, 14K white gold bracelet, circa 1960. *$1,000*
Watch courtesy of Heritage Auction Galleries

LONGINES
- Rectangular case, white dial, gold applied numerals, sub second, manual wind. *$300*

Watch courtesy of Charlie Cleves - Cleves and Lonnemann Jewelers

(Top)
LONGINES
- Square dial, manual wind, sub second, 10K yellow gold filled. *$150*

Watch courtesy of Charlie Cleves - Cleves and Lonnemann Jewelers

(Above)
LONGINES
- Rectangular case, manual wind, enameled numerals, sub second, yellow gold filled. *$200*

Watch courtesy of Charlie Cleves - Cleves and Lonnemann Jewelers

MIDO

*M*ido was founded in 1918 in the town of Biel, Switzerland, by George G. Schaeren. Mido was responsible for many firsts, such as the first automatic watch, the first center chronograph, and the smallest lady's watch to name a few.

Mido introduced the first automatic watch in 1934, called the "Multifort." Not only was the watch self-winding, but was also shock resistant, water resistant, and anti-magnetic, all firsts for wristwatch design. The center chronograph was introduced in 1945.

In 1970, Mido designed the Aquadura Crown sealing watch. The watch used a natural cork to seal the crown and therefore made it waterproof.

In the 1990s, Mido created their first Worldtime watch, which allowed the wearer to see the time anywhere in the world at the press of a button. Mido is currently owned by the Swatch Group.

(Left)
MIDO, MULTIFORT
- Enamel dial, 33mm, automatic. *$900*
  Watch courtesy of Derek Dier, WatchesToBuy.com

(Above Left)
MIDO
- Multifort, 30mm, stainless steel, 17 jewel automatic, circa 1943. *$350*
  Watch courtesy of Derek Dier, WatchesToBuy.com

(Above Right)
MIDO
- Multifort Datometer, 30mm, 17 jewel manual wind, 1940s. *$650*
  Watch courtesy of Derek Dier, WatchesToBuy.com

MOVADO

ovado was founded by Achille Ditesheim in 1881 in the town of La Chaux-de-Fonds, Switzerland.

Originally, Movado watches were all manufactured by hand. In 1889 the firm was awarded six First Class Official rating certificates. They also won a silver medal at the Universal Demonstration in Paris.

Movado launched a line of digital watches in 1930. In 1946, they began offering the "Calendomatic" watch to consumers. This watch offered the month and day markers on the dial.

Their most recognizable line, the "Museum Watch," debuted in 1969, and is still being produced today. This watch design resulted in a pairing with Andy Warhol to create one-of-a-kind watches.

Today, Movado is reproducing earlier styles, and also produces watches for brands such as Coach, Lacoste and Tommy Hilfiger.

(Above)
MOVADO
- Museum, Ref. 246-224-085, 1970s, 14K yellow gold with an integral 14K yellow gold mesh bracelet. Accompanied by a fitted box. *$750*
Image courtesy of Antiquorum Auctioneers

(Left/
MOVADO
- Museum, black dial, automatic, 14K yellow gold. *$400*
Watch courtesy of Charlie Cleves - Cleves and Lonnemann Jewelers

(Far Left)
MOVADO
- 14K yellow gold. *$400*
  Watch courtesy of Leslie Hindman Auctioneers

(Top Left)
MOVADO
- 14K yellow gold, manual wind. *$225*
  Watch courtesy of Leslie Hindman Auctioneers

(Bottom Left)
MOVADO
- Square, center seconds, circa 1960, 14K yellow gold, gold markers, gold batons, manual wind. *$300*
  Watch courtesy of Heritage Auction Galleries

(Right)
MOVADO
- Stainless steel and diamonds, quartz movement. *$250*
  Watch courtesy of Leslie Hindman Auctioneers

(Below)
MOVADO
- Stainless steel, quartz movement. *$395*
  Watch courtesy of Leslie Hindman Auctioneers

(Above)
MOVADO
- 14K yellow gold, manual wind, teardrop lugs, circa 1950s. *$600*

Watch courtesy of Chris Miller

(Left)
MOVADO FOR ABERCROMBIE & FITCH CO.
- "Shipmate," military. *$400*

Watch courtesy of Phil Lucas

MOVADO
- 14K yellow gold, gold bar markers, center sweep, manual wind, circa 1960. *$200*

Watch courtesy of Heritage Auction Galleries

MOVADO
- Kingmatic, 14K yellow gold shell, with date, circa 1960s. *$400*

Watch courtesy of James F. Dicke II

(Top Left)

MOVADO

- "Datron HS 360," chronograph, automatic, Ref. 502, 1970s. Tonneau-shaped, self-winding, water-resistant, 14K yellow gold with date, round-button chronograph, registers, tachometer and a 14K yellow gold Movado JB link bracelet. *$2,500*

Image courtesy of Antiquorum Auctioneers

(Top Middle)

MOVADO

- Chronograph, circa 1950s, 14K yellow gold, large teardrop lugs, rectangular pushers. *$3,000*

Watch courtesy of Heritage Auction Galleries

(Right)

MOVADO

- Art Deco, circa 1930, 14K gold, unique shaped lugs, ribbed top and bottom hooded bars. *$1,000*

Watch courtesy of Heritage Auction Galleries

(Below)

MOVADO

- Automatic, yellow gold-plated (40 microns) with triple date calendar and moon phases, No. 6413, case No. 498726, Ref. R 64928, 1950s. *$2,500*

Image courtesy of Antiquorum Auctioneers

OMEGA

*O*mega started life in 1880 as Louis Brandt & Son. The founding partners, brothers Louis-Paul and César Brandt had the largest Swiss watch company with an annual production of more than100,000 watches. Timepieces produced at Brandt & Son were marked Celtic, Gurzelen, Helvetia, Jura and Patria.

In 1892, they joined with Audemars Piguet to produce an exclusive minute repeater.

In 1903, banker Henri Rieckel suggested using the name "Omega." In 1909, Omega made its debut at the International ballooning contest for the Gordon Bennett Cup. In 1917, the British Royal Air Force named Omega as the watch of choice for all its squadrons. Shortly thereafter, the U.S. Army followed suit.

The Omega "Speedmaster" is one of the most collectible watches ever produced. It was introduced in 1957. NASA decided the Speedmaster Professional was its official timekeeper in 1965. In 1969, Neil Armstrong walked on the moon wearing his Omega Speedmaster Professional.

In 1983, a museum for the company was opened in Bienne, Switzerland. Omega is still producing great wristwatches today.

OMEGA
- Saint Christopher, No. 8592425, Ref. 2318, late 1930s, rare, center seconds, stainless steel. *$2,500*

Image courtesy of Antiquorum Auctioneers

(Above Left)
OMEGA
- Stainless steel, manual wind, black Roman numerals, sub second. *$125*

Watch courtesy of Phil Lucas

(Above Right)
OMEGA
- Manual wind, stainless steel, luminescent hands. *$200*

Watch courtesy of Charlie Cleves - Cleves and Lonnemann Jewelers

(Right)
OMEGA
- Manual wind, stainless steel, luminescent markers. *$125*

Watch courtesy of Phil Lucas

OMEGA,
- Tonneau-shaped, enameled numerals, sub second, manual wind, yellow gold filled. *$300*

Watch courtesy of Charlie Cleves - Cleves and Lonnemann Jewelers

OMEGA
- 14K gold, 33mm, 17 jewel manual wind, 1950s. *$1,200*

Watch courtesy of Derek Dier, WatchesToBuy.com

OMEGA
- White dial, black Roman numerals, manual wind, stainless steel. *$250*

Watch courtesy of Charlie Cleves - Cleves and Lonnemann Jewelers

HELVETIA
- 18K yellow gold, manual wind, circa 1950s. *$250*

Watch courtesy of Chris Miller

OMEGA
- Porcelain dial, sub second, enameled numerals, stainless steel. *$400*

Watch courtesy of Charlie Cleves - Cleves and Lonnemann Jewelers

(Top Left)
OMEGA
- Automatic, stainless steel, textured dial, sub second. *$125*
Watch courtesy of Phil Lucas

(Middle Left)
OMEGA
- Seamaster, black dial, automatic, stainless steel, sub second, rare. *$250*
Watch courtesy of Phil Lucas

(Below)
OMEGA
- 30T2rg manual wind, 33mm, 18K gold, 1940s. *$2,500*
Watch courtesy of Derek Dier, WatchesToBuy.com

(Above)
OMEGA
- 37.5mm, 15 jewel manual wind, circa 1939. *$1,000*
Watch courtesy of Derek Dier, WatchesToBuy.com

(Left)
OMEGA
- Oversized, 37mm, stainless steel, manual wind. *$950*
Watch courtesy of Derek Dier, WatchesToBuy.com

(Above)
OMEGA
- Automatic, silver dial, gold bar markers, date, yellow gold filled. *$200*

  Watch courtesy of Charlie Cleves - Cleves and Lonnemann Jewelers

(Far Left)
OMEGA
- Automatic, gold dial, gold markers, yellow gold filled. *$200*

  Watch courtesy of Charlie Cleves - Cleves and Lonnemann Jewelers

(Left)
OMEGA
- Automatic, day/date, silver dial, gold bar markers, yellow gold filled. *$200*

  Watch courtesy of Charlie Cleves - Cleves and Lonnemann Jewelers

(Right)
OMEGA
- Automatic, black dial, date, gold markers, yellow gold filled. *$200*

  Watch courtesy of Charlie Cleves - Cleves and Lonnemann Jewelers

(Left)
OMEGA
- Manual wind, gold dial, gold markers, sub second, yellow gold filled. *$250*

  Watch courtesy of Charlie Cleves - Cleves and Lonnemann Jewelers

(Top Right)
OMEGA
- Automatic, sub second, gold markers, silver dial, yellow gold filled. *$125*

  Watch courtesy of Phil Lucas

(Middle Right)
OMEGA
- Automatic, black dial, gold bar markers, sub second, yellow gold filled. *$125*

  Watch courtesy of Phil Lucas

(Below)
OMEGA,
- Automatic, stainless steel, sub second. *$250*

  Watch courtesy of Charlie Cleves - Cleves and Lonnemann Jewelers

(Top Left)

OMEGA

• Constellation, movement No. 17017105, Ref. 14381/2, circa 1959. Center seconds, self-winding, water-resistant, 18K pink gold with a pink gold Omega buckle. *$1,500*
Image courtesy of Antiquorum Auctioneers

(Right)

OMEGA

• Constellation, silver dial, gold bar markers, automatic, pie pan dial, 18K yellow gold. *$1,200*
Watch courtesy of Charlie Cleves - Cleves and Lonnemann Jewelers

(Bottom Far Left)

OMEGA

• Constellation, white dial, silver bar markers, automatic, date, stainless steel, pie-pan dial. *$450*
Watch courtesy of Charlie Cleves - Cleves and Lonnemann Jewelers

(Bottom Second from Left)

OMEGA

• Constellation, automatic, black dial, gold bar markers, 18K yellow gold. *$1,200*
Watch courtesy of Charlie Cleves - Cleves and Lonnemann Jewelers

(Below)

OMEGA

• Constellation "C," 24 jewel automatic, 35mm, stainless steel. *$1,000*
Watch courtesy of Derek Dier, WatchesToBuy.com

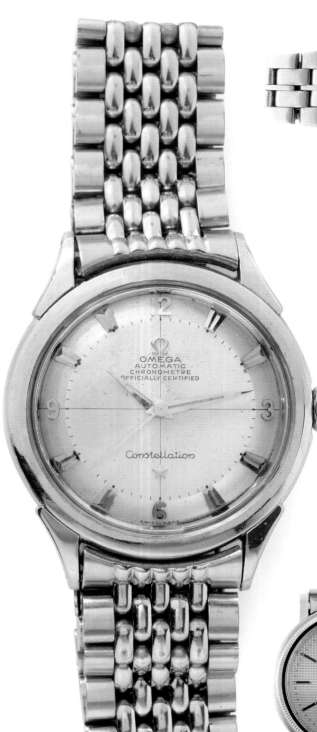

(Above)
OMEGA
- Constellation. stainless steel, day/ date, automatic.   *$300*

  Watch courtesy of Charlie Cleves - Cleves and Lonnemann Jewelers

(Left)
OMEGA
- Constellation Chronomatic, silver dial, gold markers and numbers.   *$600*

  Watch courtesy of Phil Lucas

(Bottom Middle)
OMEGA
- Constellation, electric, 36mm, stainless steel, circa 1972.   *$900*

  Watch courtesy of Derek Dier, WatchesToBuy.com

(Bottom Right)
OMEGA
- Constellation, pie-pan, kite marker dial, 24 jewel automatic, stainless steel, 1958.   *$400*

  Watch courtesy of Derek Dier, WatchesToBuy.com

(Left)
OMEGA
- Genève, gold plated, 35mm, cal. 1012 automatic. *$750*

Watch courtesy of Derek Dier, WatchesToBuy.com

(Right)
OMEGA
- Automatic, circa 1960, 18K gold screw back, Omega crown, 34 mm, water resistant. *$900*

Watch courtesy of Heritage Auction Galleries

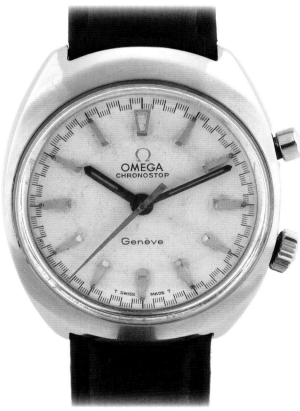

OMEGA
- Chronostop, stainless steel, 35mm, 17 jewel manual wind, 1970s. *$1,000*

Watch courtesy of Derek Dier, WatchesToBuy.com

OMEGA
- Genève, 43mm, stainless steel, automatic, 1973. *$700*

Watch courtesy of Derek Dier, WatchesToBuy.com

OMEGA
- Manual wind, gold dial, gold markers, yellow gold filled. *$150*

Watch courtesy of Charlie Cleves - Cleves and Lonnemann Jewelers

(Top Left)
OMEGA
- Seamaster Deville, 18K gold, 34.5mm, automatic, circa 1964. *$1,750*
Watch courtesy of Derek Dier, WatchesToBuy.com

(Top Middle)
OMEGA
- Seamaster, sub second, automatic, linen dial, yellow gold filled. *$200*
Watch courtesy of Charlie Cleves - Cleves and Lonnemann Jewelers

(Top Right)
OMEGA
- Circa 1960, 18K rose gold, No. 6306, snap back, long fancy curved lugs, 35 mm. *$850*
Watch courtesy of Heritage Auction Galleries

(Left)
OMEGA
- Seamaster De Ville, automatic, stainless steel, mark on back. *$250*
Watch courtesy of Phil Lucas

(Right)
OMEGA
- Seamaster, automatic, circa 1960s, large case, 18K gold screw back, Seamaster logo on back, 36 mm, wide flat bezel, heavy lugs. *$3,500*
Watch courtesy of Heritage Auction Galleries

(Above)
OMEGA
- Seamaster Deville, automatic, date, yellow gold.   *$400 (in yellow gold filled, $250)*
  Watch courtesy of Charlie Cleves - Cleves and Lonnemann Jewelers

(Top Left)
OMEGA
- Seamaster, 34mm, stainless steel, automatic.   *$750*
  Watch courtesy of Derek Dier, WatchesToBuy.com

(Bottom Left)
OMEGA
- Seamaster 600, automatic, white dial, silver bar markers, stainless steel.   *$150*
  Watch courtesy of Charlie Cleves - Cleves and Lonnemann Jewelers

(Bottom Right)
OMEGA
- Seamaster Deville, 10K yellow gold filled, quartz, date.   *$100*
  Watch courtesy of Charlie Cleves - Cleves and Lonnemann Jewelers

(Above)
OMEGA
• Constellation, calendar, yellow gold filled cap, automatic. *$450*
Watch courtesy of Charlie Cleves - Cleves and Lonnemann Jewelers

(Left)
OMEGA
• Seamaster, automatic, silver dial, date, yellow gold filled. *$250*
Watch courtesy of Charlie Cleves - Cleves and Lonnemann Jewelers

OMEGA
• Seamaster Deville, automatic, stainless steel, date. *$275*
Watch courtesy of Charlie Cleves - Cleves and Lonnemann Jewelers

OMEGA
• Seamaster, automatic, stainless steel. *$250*
Watch courtesy of Charlie Cleves - Cleves and Lonnemann Jewelers

OMEGA
• Seamaster, automatic, black dial, gold bar markers, yellow gold filled, stainless steel back. *$150*
Watch courtesy of Charlie Cleves - Cleves and Lonnemann Jewelers

OMEGA
- Automatic, bumper model, textured dial, gold bar markers, yellow gold filled. *$175*
  Watch courtesy of Charlie Cleves - Cleves and Lonnemann Jewelers

OMEGA
- Seamaster, calendar. *$250*
  Watch courtesy of Phil Lucas

OMEGA
- Automatic, yellow gold filled, silver dial, gold bar markers. *$150*
  Watch courtesy of Charlie Cleves - Cleves and Lonnemann Jewelers

OMEGA
- Seamaster, automatic, date, silver dial, silver markers, stainless steel. *$200*
  Watch courtesy of Charlie Cleves - Cleves and Lonnemann Jewelers

(Above)
OMEGA
- Seamaster, stainless steel, gold numerals. *$350*

  Watch courtesy of Phil Lucas

(Top Left)
OMEGA
- Seamaster, calendar, silver dial, gold markers, automatic, stainless steel. *$250*

  *Watch courtesy of Charlie Cleves
  - Cleves and Lonnemann Jewelers*

(Top Right)
OMEGA
- Seamaster, calendar, automatic, 35mm, stainless steel, circa 1954. *$850*

  Watch courtesy of Derek Dier, WatchesToBuy.com

OMEGA
- Seamaster, stainless steel, 3/4 size. *$300*

  Watch courtesy of Phil Lucas

OMEGA
- Seamaster, stainless steel, automatic. *$175*

  Watch courtesy of Leslie Hindman Auctioneers

(Top Left)
OMEGA
• Seamaster, automatic, gold dial,
  yellow gold cap. *$250*
  Watch courtesy of Charlie Cleves - Cleves and Lonnemann Jewelers

(Top Middle)
OMEGA
• Seamaster, 14K yellow gold filled,
  automatic, gold dial markers. *$250*
  Watch courtesy of Phil Lucas

(Top Right)
OMEGA
• Seamaster, automatic, textured dial,
  yellow gold clad. *$250*
  Watch courtesy of Phil Lucas

(Left)
OMEGA
• Ranchero, 30 mm. Ref. 2990/1, circa 1957,
  water-resistant, stainless steel. *$2,500*
  Image courtesy of Antiquorum Auctioneers

(Top Left)

OMEGA

- British military, 15 jewel manual wind, 36mm, stainless steel. *$1,650*

Watch courtesy of Derek Dier, WatchesToBuy.com

(Bottom Left)

OMEGA

- Seamaster, No. 34687672, Ref. ST 176.005, circa 1972. Self-winding, water-resistant, stainless steel with round-button chronograph, 12-hour and 60-minute registers, 24-hour indication, date and a stainless steel Omega link bracelet with deployant clasp. *$2,000*

Image courtesy of Antiquorum Auctioneers

(Bottom Middle)

OMEGA

- Seamaster, No. 35604653, Ref. 176005, circa 1970. Tonneau-shaped, self-winding, water-resistant, gold-plated and stainless steel, diver's, with round-button chronograph, registers, date, tachometer, 24-hour night/day indication and a gold-plated Omega buckle. *$1,250*

Image courtesy of Antiquorum Auctioneers

(Bottom Right)

OMEGA

- Seamaster 600, circa 1960s, screw-back case, stainless steel, back with Seamaster trademark, No. 135.011, Omega crown, angled lugs. *$700*

Watch courtesy of Heritage Auction Galleries

OMEGA
• Seamaster "Banana 200," 24 jewel automatic, 41mm, circa 1970. *$3,500*
Watch courtesy of Derek Dier, WatchesToBuy.com

OMEGA
• Seamaster Professional, automatic, date, stainless steel. *$1,000*
Watch courtesy of Charlie Cleves - Cleves and Lonnemann Jewelers

OMEGA
• Manual wind chronograph, 40mm, stainless steel. *$1,700*
Watch courtesy of Derek Dier, WatchesToBuy.com

OMEGA,
• Seamaster, 120 m/400 ft, automatic, No. 41510539, Ref. ST 166.0250, early 1970s. Tonneau-shaped, center seconds, self-winding, water-resistant, stainless steel, diver's, with date, black bezel and a stainless steel Omega mesh bracelet with slip-in clasp. *$2,500*
Image courtesy of Antiquorum Auctioneers

OMEGA
• Seamaster 200, diver's, 24 jewel automatic, 41mm, 1970. *$3,500*
Watch courtesy of Derek Dier, WatchesToBuy.com

(Top Left to Right)

OMEGA

- Speedmaster Professional, model 105012-66, stainless steel, chronograph. *$4,000*

  Watch courtesy of Charlie Cleves - Cleves and Lonnemann Jewelers

OMEGA

- "Pre-Moon" Speedmaster ST 105-003, chronograph, circa 1965, screw back with engraved Seamaster logo, steel, round pushers, crown with no guard, manual wind. *$2,600*

  Watch courtesy of Heritage Auction Galleries

OMEGA

- Speedmaster Professional, in stainless steel. *$2,500*

  Watch courtesy of Leslie Hindman Auctioneers

OMEGA

- Speedmaster Professional, Ref. 186.0004, circa 1980. Water-resistant, quartz with LCD digital display for the round-button chronograph functions, date, day of the week and an integral stainless steel Omega link bracelet with deployant clasp. Accompanied by the original box and instructions. *$1,500*

  Image courtesy of Antiquorum Auctioneers

(Right)

OMEGA

- Apollo XI Speedmaster Professional, No. 28080634, Ref. 145022-69, 1969. Water-resistant, 18K yellow gold with round-button chronograph, registers, tachometer and an 18K yellow gold Omega link bracelet. *$13,000*

  Image courtesy of Antiquorum Auctioneers

(Top Left)
OMEGA
- Speedmaster, automatic, 42.5mm, stainless steel, 1970s. *$2,000*
  Watch courtesy of Derek Dier, WatchesToBuy.com

(Bottom Left)
OMEGA
- "Speedy 125," limited-edition chronograph, 1973, stainless steel, sapphire crystal, black tachymetre bezel, screw back with Seamaster logo, center sweep, automatic. Note: The "Speedy 125," as it's known to collectors, is a chronometer-rated chronograph produced in a limited number of 2,000 to celebrate the 125th anniversary of the founding of Omega. *$1,200*
  Watch courtesy of Heritage Auction Galleries

(Bottom Middle)
OMEGA
- Speedmaster, three-register chronograph, stainless steel, automatic. *$1,300*
  Watch courtesy of Charlie Cleves - Cleves and Lonnemann Jewelers

(Below)
OMEGA
- Speedmaster, automatic, stainless steel, circa 1980s. *$1,200*
  Watch courtesy of Chris Miller

(Top Left)

OMEGA

- Flightmaster, No. 33310189, Ref. ST
  145.026, 1972. Tonneau-shaped, two time
  zones, water-resistant, stainless steel,
  aviator's, with four hands and three crowns,
  round-button chronograph, 12-hour
  and 30-minute registers, and a stainless
  steel Omega link bracelet. *$2,500*

Image courtesy of Antiquorum Auctioneersv

(Bottom Left to Right)

OMEGA

- Flightmaster, circa 1972, stainless steel,
  hooded lugs, screw back with airplane logo,
  round push buttons, manual wind. *$1,900*

Watch courtesy of Heritage Auction Galleries

OMEGA

- Tropical Dial, movement No. 19583904, Ref.
  ST 105.002-62, 1963. Water-resistant, stainless
  steel with round-button chronograph,
  registers, tachometer and a stainless steel
  Omega link bracelet. Accompanied by
  a fitted box, Certificate of Authenticity
  and a spare JB bracelet. *$8,000*

Image courtesy of Antiquorum Auctioneers

OMEGA

- Aviator's, No. 9312459, case No. 9532084,
  1940s. "Staybrite" stainless steel, with
  elapsed-time indication. *$7,500*

Image courtesy of Antiquorum Auctioneers

(Top Left)
OMEGA
- Automatic, moon phase and calendar, circa 1990, 18K yellow gold, display back.   *$5,000*
  Watch courtesy of Heritage Auction Galleries

(Top Right)
OMEGA
- Chronograph, No. 12976788, Ref. 2279-3, late 1950s. "Staybrite" stainless steel with square-button chronograph, registers and tachometer.   *$3,000*
  Image courtesy of Antiquorum Auctioneers

(Far Left)
OMEGA
- Cosmic, movement No. 11204897, Ref. No. 2486-2, 1950s. Pink gold-plated with triple date and moon phases.   *$1,500*
  Image courtesy of Antiquorum Auctioneers

(Left)
OMEGA
- Speedsonic Lobster, 300 Hz, Ref. ST 188.0001 / 388.0800, circa 1975. Stainless steel, electronic with square-button chronograph, 12-hour and 30-minute registers, tachometer, day, date and an integral Omega stainless steel link bracelet with deployant clasp.   *$1,250*
  Image courtesy of Antiquorum Auctioneers

(Top from Left to Right
OMEGA

- Manual wind, square dial, diamond markers, 14K yellow gold. *$400*
  Watch courtesy of Charlie Cleves - Cleves and Lonnemann Jewelers

OMEGA

- Automatic, No. 15899881, case No. 198481, Ref. 3971 SC, circa 1957. Square, center seconds, antimagnetic, self-winding, 18K pink gold. Accompanied by a fitted box. *$2,000*
  Image courtesy of Antiquorum Auctioneers

OMEGA

- Constellation Mega Quartz, circa 1973, 18K yellow gold, polished and brushed finish, water resistant, applied gold bar markers, date at 6. *$3,000*
  Watch courtesy of Heritage Auction Galleries

(Bottom from Left to Right)
OMEGA

- Circa 1970s, 14K white gold, brushed finish, Omega crown, manual wind. *$500*
  Watch courtesy of Heritage Auction Galleries

OMEGA

- Circa 1940s, 14K gold, Art Deco-style lugs, sub-seconds, Arabic numerals, manual wind. *$600*
  Watch courtesy of Heritage Auction Galleries

(Top Left to Right)
OMEGA
- 18K white gold and diamonds, manual wind, 18K white gold bracelet, circa 1980. *$1,500*

Watch courtesy of Heritage Auction Galleries

OMEGA
- Lady's Constellation, circa 1995, stainless steel, diamond and gold bezel, automatic movement. *$1,075*

Watch courtesy of Heritage Auction Galleries

(Bottom Left to Right)
OMEGA
- Constellation, circa 1970, 18K yellow gold, snap back with Constellation logo, bezel set with diamonds. *$3,300*

Watch courtesy of Heritage Auction Galleries

OMEGA
- Lady's, gold and opal bracelet, circa 1975, 14K yellow gold, scalloped bezel, manual wind. *$2,100*

Watch courtesy of Heritage Auction Galleries

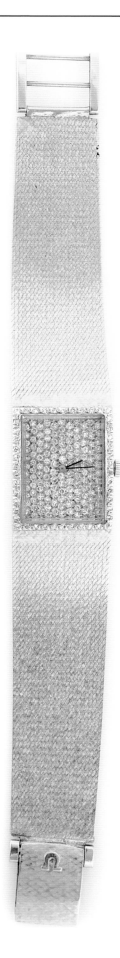

(Right)
OMEGA
- 18K yellow gold. *$550*
  Watch courtesy of Leslie Hindman Auctioneers

(Below)
OMEGA
- Automatic with integral band, circa 1970s, 14K yellow gold, black bar markers and batons, 14K yellow gold band. *$1,250*
  Watch courtesy of Heritage Auction Galleries

(Above)
OMEGA
- Circa 1970s, 14K yellow gold, tonneau-shaped, full diamond bezel, No. 315850. *$1,075*
  Watch courtesy of Heritage Auction Galleries

(Left)
OMEGA
- 14K yellow gold and diamonds. *$3,000*
  Watch courtesy of Leslie Hindman Auctioneers

(Above)
OMEGA
- 18K yellow gold and diamonds, manual wind. *$900*

  Watch courtesy of Leslie Hindman Auctioneers

(Right)
OMEGA
- Constellation, circa 1970s, 18K yellow gold, two body, 36 mm, tiger-eye set crown, stepped bezel. *$2,100*

  Watch courtesy of Heritage Auction Galleries

(Below)
OMEGA
- Lady's, quartz movement. *$200*

  Watch courtesy of Leslie Hindman Auctioneers

PATEK PHILIPPE

*I*n 1839, Antoine Norbert de Patek and Francois Czapek founded Patek, Czapek & Co. in Geneva. They were known for producing high-caliber timepieces in limited quantities.

By 1845, Czapek left the company and Patek offered the position of technical director to a young watchmaker, Jean-Adrien Philippe, whom he met at a Paris exhibition. The company was renamed Patek Philippe & Co. in 1851.

Patek Philippe was the creator of the first wristwatch in 1867. Originally thought to be a woman's accessory instead of a man's, many wristwatches were worn on the wrist with a head attached to a silk ribbon. One of the most recognizable clients of Patek Philippe watches was Queen Victoria of England.

At the 1867 Paris Exhibition, Patek Philippe was exhibiting chronographs, and also watches offering perpetual calendars, repeaters and split-second chronographs.

Not only was Patek Philippe responsible for the first wristwatch, they also created the free mainspring and the sweep secondhand. The company was also known for their engraving work and enameling. After 150+ years, Patek Philippe is still a leading Swiss watch company, producing fine clocks, wristwatches and pocket watches.

PATEK PHILIPPE & CIE, GENÈVE
- No. 961863, case No. 639954, Ref. 565, 1948. Water-resistant, stainless steel with deployant clasp. Accompanied by the Extract from the Archives. (An "Extract from the Archives" states the information kept up to date in the Patek Philippe archive registers since 1839. It can be ordered for any Patek Philippe watch older than five years.) *$17,500*

Image courtesy of Antiquorum Auctioneers

PATEK PHILIPPE
- Ref. 5000, circa 1990s, 18K yellow gold, sapphire crystals, automatic movement. *$10,750*

Watch courtesy of Heritage Auction Galleries

(Top Left)

PATEK PHILIPPE & CIE, GENÈVE

- No. 1220969, case No. 2733316, Ref. 3537, 1970s, 18K yellow gold with an 18K yellow gold Patek Philippe buckle.   *$2,500*

  Image courtesy of Antiquorum Auctioneers

(Top Middle)

PATEK PHILIPPE

- Circa 1940, 18K rose gold, teardrop lugs, manual wind.   *$4,000*

  Watch courtesy of Heritage Auction Galleries

(Top Right)

PATEK PHILIPPE

- "Convertible" case, circa 1960, Ref. 3419, stainless steel, silver dial with incised hour markers, manual wind. (This rare case design was developed to give the owner the option of having a watch with traditional lugs and a leather strap or a metal bracelet which would fit the watch with an "integral" look. Fewer than 10 Ref. 3419 models have appeared on the market in the past two decades.)   *$15,000*

  Watch courtesy of Heritage Auction Galleries

(Left)

PATEK PHILIPPE & CIE, GENÈVE, NAUTILUS

- No. 1507521, Ref. 3770, circa 1985. Oval, water-resistant, 18K yellow gold quartz with an 18K yellow gold Patek Philippe buckle. Accompanied by a fitted box and certificate of origin.   *$6,500*

  Image courtesy of Antiquorum Auctioneers

PATEK PHILIPPE
- Genève, movement No. 704125, case No. 307194, Ref. 570, circa 1955. Large, center seconds, 18K pink gold. Accompanied by an Extract from the Archives. (An "Extract from the Archives" states the information kept up to date in the Patek Philippe archive registers since 1839. It can be ordered for any Patek Philippe watch older than five years.) *$25,000*

Image courtesy of Antiquorum Auctioneers

(Above)
PATEK PHILIPPE
- 18K yellow gold, Ref. 1491, Breguet balance spring, circa 1950. *$13,000*

Watch courtesy of Heritage Auction Galleries

(Bottom Left)
PATEK PHILIPPE
- Genève, movement No. 720638, case No. 667417, Ref. 2455, circa 1945, 18K yellow gold with an 18K yellow gold Patek Philippe buckle. *$10,000*

Image courtesy of Antiquorum Auctioneers

(Bottom Middle)
PATEK PHILIPPE FOR TIFFANY
- Circa 1955, with rare Masonic dial. *$3,000*

Watch courtesy of Heritage Auction Galleries

PATEK PHILIPPE
- 18K yellow gold, "Calatrava," manual wind, circa 1950. *$3,000*

  Watch courtesy of Heritage Auction Galleries

PATEK PHILIPPE
- Ref. 2591/1, circa 1962, 18K yellow gold, teardrop lugs, original crown, manual wind. *$4,100*

  Watch courtesy of Heritage Auction Galleries

PATEK PHILIPPE
- Genève, No. 1124884, case No. 320936, Ref. 3541, 1960s. Self-winding, water-resistant, 18K yellow gold with date. Accompanied by a Patek Philippe fitted box. *$8,500*

  Image courtesy of Antiquorum Auctioneers

PATEK PHILIPPE
- Genève, No. 701501, case No. 666948, Ref. 1578, circa 1952, 18K yellow gold, center seconds. *$7,500*

  Image courtesy of Antiquorum Auctioneers

PATEK PHILIPPE
- Ref. 2592-1, circa 1965, 18K yellow gold, fancy curved lugs, manual wind. *$2,300*

  Watch courtesy of Heritage Auction Galleries

PATEK PHILIPPE
- Ref. 2595/1, circa 1961, 18K yellow gold, No. 2623729, manual wind. *$4,400*

  Watch courtesy of Heritage Auction Galleries

(Above)

PATEK PHILIPPE

- Genève, Pink Banana, movement No. 972441, case No. 659874, Ref. 2442, 1950. Rounded flared "bombé" lugs, 18K pink gold with an 18K pink gold Patek Philippe buckle. Accompanied by the Extract from the Archives. (An "Extract from the Archives" states the information kept up to date in the Patek Philippe archive registers since 1839. It can be ordered for any Patek Philippe watch older than five years.) *$50,000*

Image courtesy of Antiquorum Auctioneers

(Left)

PATEK PHILIPPE

- Top Hat, circa 1946, 18K yellow gold, Ref. 1450, hooded and extended lugs, 38mm x 21mm, manual wind. *$6,500*

Watch courtesy of Heritage Auction Galleries

(Right)

PATEK PHILIPPE

- Top Hat, circa 1940s, 18K rose gold, hooded lugs, sub seconds. *$6,500*

Watch courtesy of Heritage Auction Galleries

(Above)
PATEK PHILIPPE & CIE, GENÈVE
• No. 1143305, case No. 2666906, Ref. 3557, 1970s. Rectangular, curved, 18K yellow gold with an 18K yellow gold Patek Philippe buckle. Accompanied by a fitted box.   *$5,000*
Image courtesy of Antiquorum Auctioneers

(Top Right)
PATEK PHILIPPE & CIE, GENÈVE
• No. 973898, case No. 668204, Ref. 425, circa 1950. Rectangular, curved, 18K yellow gold with an 18K yellow gold Patek Philippe buckle. Accompanied by a fitted box.   *$9,000*
Image courtesy of Antiquorum Auctioneers

(Above)
PATEK PHILIPPE
• Manual wind, diamond bezel, 18K yellow gold, Ref. 4385, circa 1970s. *$4,400*
Watch courtesy of Tim and Reyne Haines

(Left)
PATEK PHILIPPE
• 18K yellow gold, manual wind. *$9,000*
Watch courtesy of Leslie Hindman Auctioneers

(Right)

PATEK PHILIPPE & CIE, GENÈVE

• No. 1284328, case No. 521640, Ref. 3591-1, 1970s. Thin, self-winding, 18K yellow gold with an integral 18K yellow gold Patek Philippe textured mesh bracelet. Accompanied by a fitted box.   *$7,000*

Image courtesy of Antiquorum Auctioneers

(Bottom from Left to Right)

PATEK PHILIPPE & CO.

• 18K yellow gold diamond and emerald covered dial, 18K yellow gold mesh bracelet, circa 1957.   *$10,000*

Watch courtesy of Heritage Auction Galleries

PATEK PHILIPPE & CIE

• Genève, lady's Tiger Eye, No. 1410289, Ref. 4283/1, circa 1980, 18K yellow gold, with an integrated Patek Philippe yellow gold three-strand woven chain bracelet.   *$5,000*

Image courtesy of Antiquorum Auctioneers

PATEK PHILIPPE & CIE

• Genève, lady's Nautilus, Ref. 4700, circa 1985. Water-resistant, 18K yellow gold and diamonds, quartz, with date, yellow gold integrated bracelet and white gold deployant clasp.   *$6,500*

Image courtesy of Antiquorum Auctioneers

(Above)
PATEK PHILIPPE
- 18K white gold and diamonds, blue dial with diamond numeral indicators, diamond bezel, manual wind, mesh band with deployant clasp. *$4,500*

Watch courtesy of Skinner Inc.

(Right)
PATEK PHILIPPE & CIE, GENÈVE
- Retailed by Beyer, No. 791929, case No. 2615230, Ref. 3401, 1962. Unusual platinum and diamonds, with a detachable Gay Frères platinum link bracelet. *$25,000*

Image courtesy of Antiquorum Auctioneers

(Far Right)
PATEK PHILIPPE
- Art Deco, 18K white gold and diamonds. *$6,700*

Watch courtesy of Leslie Hindman Auctioneers

(Top Left to Right)
PATEK PHILIPPE

- Ref. 3445/6, circa 1968, 18K white gold, date at 3, diamond baguette and round hour markers, sub seconds, automatic, 18K gold rotor, 18K white gold band, boxes included. *$6,500*
Watch courtesy of Heritage Auction Galleries

PATEK PHILIPPE

- Lady's, circa 1968, 18K white gold, applied bar markers, manual wind. *$1,500*
Watch courtesy of Heritage Auction Galleries

(Bottom Left to Right)
PATEK PHILIPPE

- Lady's, circa 1950s, 18K yellow gold, applied gold bar markers, manual wind, 14K yellow gold band. *$1,250*
Watch courtesy of Heritage Auction Galleries

PATEK PHILIPPE

- Lady's, circa 1965, 18K yellow gold, Ref. 3266/60, manual wind. *$1,600*
Watch courtesy of Heritage Auction Galleries

PIAGET

eorges Piaget began making watch movements in his hometown of La Côte-aux-Fées, Switzerland, in 1874. His movements attracted the attention of some of the most prestigious watchmakers in Switzerland.

It was not until the early 1940s did Piaget begin manufacturing complete. Piaget struck gold when they began creating watch dials out of fine gems, such as lapis and onyx.

(Top from Left to Right)
PIAGET
- 14K yellow gold, waterproof, self-winding, original box, circa 1962. *$2,000*
  Watch courtesy of Heritage Auction Galleries

PIAGET
- Tank, circa 1980s, 18K gold, quartz. *$650*
  Watch courtesy of Heritage Auction Galleries

(Bottom)
PIAGET
- 1902 $20 coin, manual wind, 18K yellow gold. *$1,900*
  Watch courtesy of Leslie Hindman Auctioneers

PIAGET
- 18K yellow gold and tiger eye. *$2,400*

Watch courtesy of Leslie Hindman Auctioneers

PIAGET
- 18K white gold and tiger eye, manual wind, circa 1970s. *$1,000*

Watch courtesy of Leslie Hindman Auctioneers

PIAGET
- 18K white gold and diamonds, manual wind. *$7,800*

Watch courtesy of Leslie Hindman Auctioneers

PIAGET
- 18K white gold with diamonds, manual wind, circa 1970. *$1,750*

Watch courtesy of Heritage Auction Galleries

PIAGET
- "Esclave," 18K white gold and diamonds, lapis lazuli dial, 18K white gold bracelet, circa 1970. *$21,000*

Watch courtesy of Heritage Auction Galleries

(Above)
PIAGET
- 18K gold, basket-weave dial with baton numeral indicators, manual-wind, basket-weave strap, dated 1968.   *$2,750*

  Watch courtesy of Skinner Inc.

(Top Left)
PIAGET
- Emperador, circa 1980, 18K gold with integral bracelet, 24 mm, No. 382297, water resistant, quartz movement. *$5,600*

  Watch courtesy of Heritage Auction Galleries

(Far Right)
PIAGET
- 18K yellow gold. *$2,750*

  Watch courtesy of Leslie Hindman Auctioneers

(Right)
PIAGET
- Lady's Polo, circa 1990, 18K yellow gold, Ref. 8131 G701, quartz movement. *$2,500*

  Watch courtesy of Heritage Auction Galleries

(Bottom Right)
PIAGET
- 18K yellow gold, manual wind. *$1,400*

  Watch courtesy of Leslie Hindman Auctioneers

(Top Left)
PIAGET
- Lady's, circa 1980, 18K yellow gold, with integral Piaget bracelet, Florentine finish, full diamond bezel, quartz movement.   *$3,800*
  Watch courtesy of Heritage Auction Galleries

(Top Middle)
PIAGET
- 18K yellow gold and diamonds.   *$1,200*
  Watch courtesy of Leslie Hindman Auctioneers

(Top Right)
PIAGET
- 18K yellow gold diamond and sapphire, lapis lazuli dial, manual wind, circa 1980.   *$2,250*
  Watch courtesy of Heritage Auction Galleries

(Below)
PIAGET
- 18K yellow gold, dual time with textured round dial holding two small round gold dials with black hands and baton numerals, each with 17-jewel movements, with integrated textured mesh bracelet. Dial, movements, case and buckle signed Piaget.   *$3,360*
  Watch courtesy of Leslie Hindman Auctioneers

ROLEX

*R*olex was founded in London 1908 by a German, Hans Wilsdorf. Originally, the firm was named Wilsdorf & Davis. Davis was Wilsdorf's brother-in-law. In the early years, the company worked with Aegler, a Swiss company, to provide movements for their wristwatch designs.

It wasn't until 1910 that Rolex submitted their first movement to the School of Horology in Switzerland. In 1914, London's Kew Observatory certified a Rolex watch to be as precise as a marine chronometer. This was the first time a watch had received a chronometer rating.

Wristwatches had several challenges to overcome. Many were not accurate, nor were they reliable. The chronometer award proved Rolex watches to be accurate.

The next hurdle to overcome for watchmakers was making a watch waterproof. Rolex was able to design a new screw-down crown and casebook that would eliminate moisture seepage. To prove their watches were waterproof, Rolex placed their watches submerged in filled aquariums in watch shops around the world. The model was named "Oyster." Wilsdorf chose the name after experiencing difficulty opening an oyster at dinner one evening.

(Far Left)
ROLEX
- Paul Newman Oyster Cosmograph, Ref. 6263, circa 1973. Water-resistant, stainless steel with black bezel, round-button chronograph, registers, tachometer and a stainless steel Rolex Oyster bracelet. Accompanied by a fitted box. *$75,000*
Image courtesy of Antiquorum Auctioneers

(Left)
ROLEX
- Oyster Cosmograph, Color Change Daytona, Ref. 6263. Made circa 1975. Water-resistant, stainless steel with black bezel, round-button chronograph, registers, tachometer and a stainless steel Rolex buckle. Accompanied by a fitted box and instruction booklets. *$45,000*
Image courtesy of Antiquorum Auctioneers

While promoting the "Oyster" in aquariums brought brand awareness to Rolex, Wilsdorf was looking for other opportunities. He learned of a British woman who was planning to swim across the English Channel. Wilsdorf provided her with an "Oyster" and hired a photographer to follow her trek. As she emerged from the channel, her watch had remained waterproof. Wilsdorf then took out a front page ad in the London Daily Mail stating: "The Wonder Watch that Defies the Elements: Moisture Proof, Waterproof, Heat Proof, Vibration Proof, Cold Proof, Dust Proof."

In 1931, Rolex developed the "Rotor," the first automatic movement. This movement offered a metal plate that would rotate internally as the wearer moved their arm. This would keep the watch wound. The model was called the "Perpetual."

By World War II, Rolex had become the timepiece of choice for the British Royal Air Force. Pilots snubbed the government-issued watches for the more prestigious Rolex "Oyster Perpetual" model. Rolex, in turn, offered any British prisoner of war whose Rolex watch had been confiscated a free replacement.

Wilsdorf died in 1960 and in 1962, the company's board of directors appointed André Heiniger as the new managing director. Heiniger had worked under Wilsdorf for 12 years and had a similar vision in mind for the Rolex brand.

With the arrival of the Japanese quartz watches on the market, numerous Swiss factories closed. While Rolex eventually developed a quartz watch, it remained a small fraction of its overall business.

Rolex produces approximately 650,000 watches every year.

(Top from Left to Right)
ROLEX
- Bubble Back, circa 1937, stainless steel, with rose gold bezel, ref. 3772, Roman and Arabic luminescent numerals, hooded lugs, automatic. *$5,000*
  Watch courtesy of Heritage Auction Galleries

ROLEX
- Bubble Back, two tone, Roman numeral dial, manual wind, circa 1940s. *$2,800*
  Watch courtesy of James F. Dicke II

(Bottom Right)
ROLEX
- Oyster Perpetual, day/date, Ref. 1803, in 1972. Center seconds, self-winding, water-resistant, 18K pink gold with day and date and an 18K pink gold Rolex clasp. *$17,500*
  Image courtesy of Antiquorum Auctioneers

(Below)
ROLEX
- Oyster Perpetual, date, silver dial, gold markers, automatic, 14K yellow gold. *$1,600*
  Watch courtesy of Charlie Cleves - Cleves and Lonnemann Jewelers

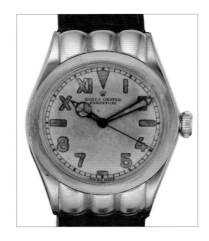

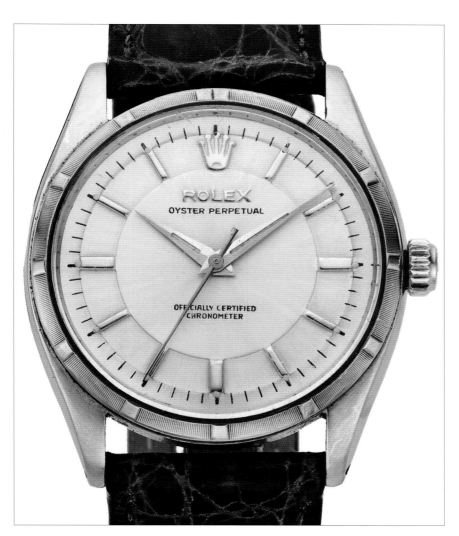

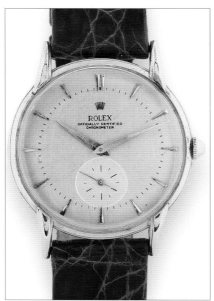

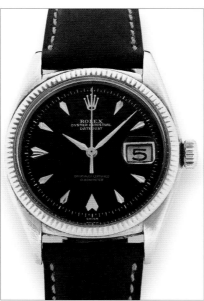

(Top Left)
ROLEX

- Oyster Perpetual, circa 1940, stainless steel with gold bezel, Ref. 6565, case no. 84068, automatic movement. *$1,900*
  Watch courtesy of Heritage Auction Galleries

(Top Right)
ROLEX

- Oyster Perpetual, date, Ref. 1803, circa 1960. Center seconds, self-winding, water-resistant, 18K yellow gold. *$4,000*
  Image courtesy of Antiquorum Auctioneers

(Far Left)
ROLEX

- Ref. 4816, circa 1951, 18K yellow gold with a gold-plated Rolex buckle. *$2,500*
  Image courtesy of Antiquorum Auctioneers

(Left)
ROLEX

- Genève, Oyster Perpetual, Datejust, Ref. 6305, circa 1953. Black dial, center seconds, water-resistant, self-winding, 18K yellow gold chronometer with date. *$6,000*
  Image courtesy of Antiquorum Auctioneers

(Top Right)
ROLEX

- Oyster Perpetual Metropolitan, Meritus, 34mm, gold capped 25 jewel automatic, Canadian issue.   *$4,500*
  Watch courtesy of Derek Dier, WatchesToBuy.com

(Below)
ROLEX

- Circa 1950, 18K rose gold, snap back, Rolex crown on winder, tapered lugs, 36 mm, manual wind.   *$5,300*
  Watch courtesy of Heritage Auction Galleries

(Bottom Middle)
ROLEX

- Oyster Perpetual, automatic, white dial, gold markers, gold shell.   *$1,000*
  Watch courtesy of Charlie Cleves - Cleves and Lonnemann Jewelers

(Bottom Right)
ROLEX

- Oyster, date, Ref. 1550, circa 1972, gold shell with smooth bezel, gold screw-down Oyster crown, stainless steel case back.   *$1,600*
  Watch courtesy of Heritage Auction Galleries

(Left)
ROLEX
- Oyster Perpetual, date, gold dial, gold markers, automatic, gold shell. *$1,100*
Watch courtesy of Charlie Cleves - Cleves and Lonnemann Jewelers

(Right Top from Left to Right)
ROLEX
- Oyster, stainless steel, automatic, replacement band. *$700*
Watch courtesy of Leslie Hindman Auctioneers

ROLEX
- Oyster Perpetual, Air-King, silver dial, silver markers, stainless steel. *$900*
Watch courtesy of Charlie Cleves - Cleves and Lonnemann Jewelers

(Right Bottom)
ROLEX
- Oyster Perpetual, automatic, gold dial, gold markers, 18K yellow gold. *$2,400*
Watch courtesy of Charlie Cleves - Cleves and Lonnemann Jewelers

(Below)
ROLEX
- Oyster Speedking, stainless steel. *$500*
Watch courtesy of Phil Lucas

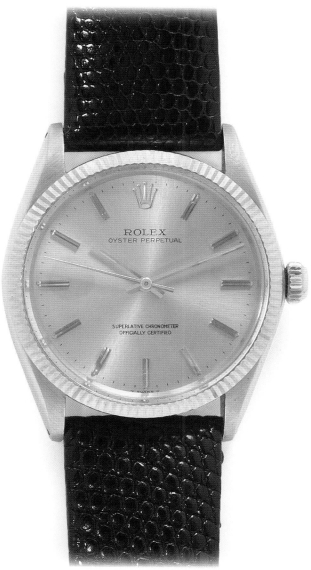

(Left from Top to Bottom)
ROLEX

• Datejust, circa 1978, Ref. 16013, two-tone stainless steel with fluted gold bezel, gold crown, automatic movement. *$1,900*
Watch courtesy of Heritage Auction Galleries

ROLEX

• Oyster Perpetual, circa 1972, stainless steel, Ref. 1002, No. 3409984, smooth bezel, automatic movement. *$1,075*
Watch courtesy of Heritage Auction Galleries

ROLEX

• Datejust in two-tone 14K rose gold and stainless steel with Jubilee. *$3,200*
Watch courtesy of Tim and Reyne Haines

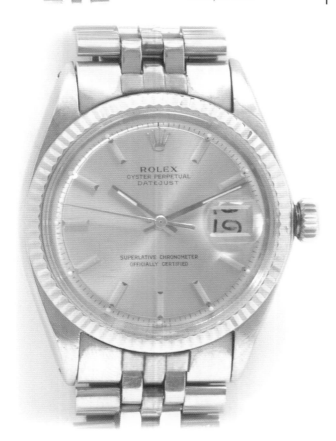

(Above)
ROLEX

• Oyster Perpetual, Datejust, with "Super-Oyster" crown, Ref. 6075, circa 1950. Tonneau-shaped, center-seconds, self-winding, water-resistant, 18K yellow gold with date and an 18K yellow gold Rolex Jubilee bracelet. *$5,000*
Image courtesy of Antiquorum Auctioneers

(Left)
ROLEX

• Oyster Perpetual, Datejust, two-tone jubilee band, circa 1970s. *$2,500*
Watch courtesy of Chris Miller

(Top from Left to Right)
ROLEX

- Datejust, stainless steel, stretch rivet band, 1958. *$1,400*

Watch courtesy of Tim and Reyne Haines

ROLEX

- Oyster, date, circa 1977, mid-size stainless steel, smooth bezel, automatic movement. *$1,000*

Watch courtesy of Heritage Auction Galleries

ROLEX

- Early Oyster Perpetual, circa 1968, 18K yellow gold, fluted bezel, automatic movement. *$3,800*

Watch courtesy of Heritage Auction Galleries

(Bottom Right)
ROLEX

- Chronograph, pre-Daytona, black dial, Ref. 6238, 1960s. Water-resistant, stainless steel with round-button chronograph, registers, tachometer, stainless steel riveted Rolex Oyster bracelet with deployant clasp. *$50,000*

Image courtesy of Antiquorum Auctioneers

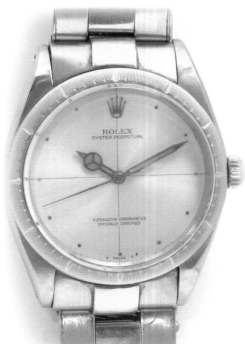

(Top Left)
ROLEX
- President, circa 1995, 18K gold, fluted bezel, automatic movement. *$5,975*
  Watch courtesy of Heritage Auction Galleries

(Bottom Left)
ROLEX
- Oyster Perpetual, Zephyr, 14K rose gold and stainless steel with original rivet band, circa 1950s. *$2,400*
  Watch courtesy of Tim and Reyne Haines

(Bottom Right)
ROLEX
- President, 18K yellow gold, automatic, day/date. *$10,000*
  Watch courtesy of James F. Dicke II

(Below)
ROLEX
- Date, model 1530, circa 1985 (quartz date-style case) in stainless steel, automatic movement.   *$7,500*
  Watch courtesy of Tim and Reyne Haines

(Above)
ROLEX
- Air-King, date, 35mm, stainless steel, 25 jewel automatic.   *$3,000*
  Watch courtesy of Derek Dier, WatchesToBuy.com

(Left from Top to Bottom)
ROLEX
- Stainless steel, date, circa 1960, manual wind.   *$1,100*
  Watch courtesy of Phil Lucas

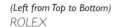

ROLEX
- Date in stainless steel, Oyster band, circa 1989.   *$1,600*
  Watch courtesy of Tim and Reyne Haines

(Bottom from Left to Right)

ROLEX
- Oyster Perpetual, date, Submariner, Panama Canal, No. 67/75, Ref. 16610. Made in a limited edition of 75 pieces in 1999. Center seconds, self-winding, water resistant, stainless steel, diver's, with a stainless steel Rolex Fliplock Oyster bracelet. *$25,000*

Image courtesy of Antiquorum Auctioneers

ROLEX
- Oyster Perpetual, date, Sea-Dweller 4000ft = 1220m, Ref. 16660. Made in 1984. Center seconds, self-winding, water-resistant, stainless steel, diver's, with second-generation helium-escape valve, date and a stainless steel Rolex Oyster Fliplock bracelet. *$5,000*

Image courtesy of Antiquorum Auctioneers

ROLEX
- Submariner in stainless steel, model 16800, Oyster flip-lock band, circa 1995. *$4,200*

Watch courtesy of Tim and Reyne Haines

ROLEX
- Sea-Dweller Submariner, Double Red model 1680, circa 1971. *$28,000*

Watch courtesy of Tim and Reyne Haines

ROLEX

- **GMT Master**, stainless steel, circa 1966, gilt gloss dial, automatic.   *$6,000*

Watch courtesy of Tim and Reyne Haines

(Left)
ROLEX

- **GMT Master 1675**, stainless steel, 1972 rivet band, "Pepsi" bezel.   *$5,500*

Watch courtesy of Tim and Reyne Haines

(Bottom Right)
ROLEX

- **GMT Master I**, stainless steel, jubilee band.   *$13,000*

Watch courtesy of Phil Lucas

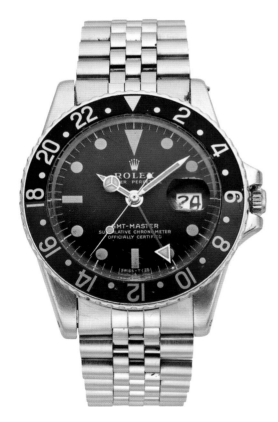

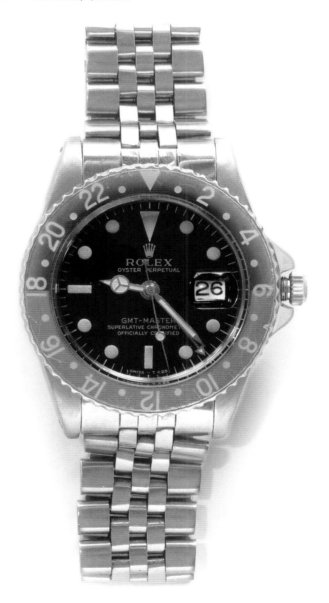

ROLEX

- **GMT Master**, circa 1971, Ref. 1675, stainless steel, red and blue bi-directional 24-hour bezel, automatic movement.   *$3,500*

Watch courtesy of Heritage Auction Galleries

(Top from Left to Right)
ROLEX
- Submariner, circa 1962, Ref. 5513, rotating black bezel, stainless steel, automatic movement. *$3,300*
Watch courtesy of Heritage Auction Galleries

ROLEX
- Explorer I, model 1016, stainless steel, circa 1994. *$5,500*
Watch courtesy of Tim and Reyne Haines

(Below)
ROLEX
- Steve McQueen Oyster Perpetual, date, Explorer II, Ref. 1655, in 1979. Center seconds, self-winding, water-resistant, stainless steel with date, special 24-hour bezel, large white arrow 24-hour hand and a stainless steel Rolex Oyster bracelet. Accompanied by a fitted box, hangtag and instruction booklets. *$17,500*
Image courtesy of Antiquorum Auctioneers

ROLEX
- Submariner, Ref. 5513, in stainless steel with rivet band, circa 1972. *$5,500*
Watch courtesy of Tim and Reyne Haines

(Top Left)
ROLEX

• Bubble Back, automatic,
  14K yellow gold, 24-hour
  dial, circa 1940s. *$4,500*

  Watch courtesy of James F. Dicke II

(Top Right)
ROLEX

• Corvette, Canadian issue,
  WWII, 17 jewel manual
  wind, rare. *$3,500*

  Watch courtesy of Derek Dier, WatchesToBuy.com

(Bottom Left)
ROLEX

• Oyster, Royalite, Canadian
  WWII, 17 jewel manual
  wind, circa 1940. *$2,750*

  Watch courtesy of Derek Dier, WatchesToBuy.com

(Bottom Middle)
ROLEX

• Skyrocket, Canadian WWII,
  30mm, sterling silver,
  17 jewel manual wind,
  circa 1942. *$2,250*

  Watch courtesy of Derek Dier, WatchesToBuy.com

(Top Right)
ROLEX

- Hurricane Observatory, Canadian issue, WWII, 17 jewel manual wind, rare. *$3,500*
  Watch courtesy of Derek Dier, WatchesToBuy.com

(Bottom Left)
ROLEX

- Oyster, Royal Canadian, WWII, 30mm, stainless steel, 17 jewel. *$2,250*
  Watch courtesy of Derek Dier, WatchesToBuy.com

(Bottom Middle)
ROLEX

- Oyster Perpetual, Bubble Back, sub second, automatic, pink gold and stainless. *$2,200*
  Watch courtesy of Tim and Reyne Haines

(Bottom Right)
ROLEX

- Oyster Perpetual, Bubble Back, Ref. 6052, black dial, stainless steel. *$1,500*
  Watch courtesy of Phil Lucas

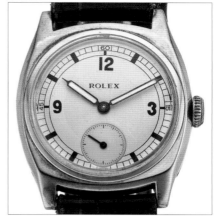

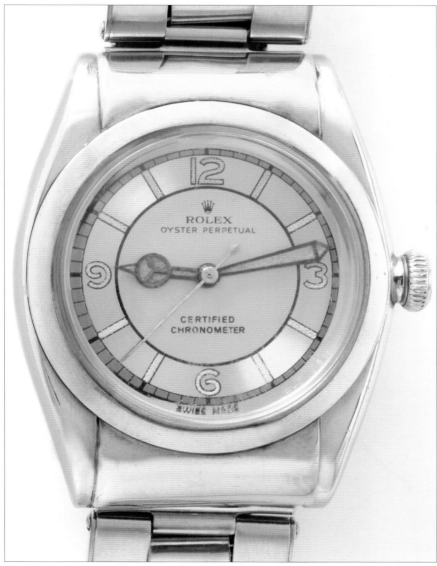

ROLEX

- Oyster Perpetual, Bubble Back, case No. 474355, Ref. 3131, circa 1946. Tonneau-shaped, self-winding, water-resistant, center seconds, 14K pink gold with a yellow-gold-plated Rolex buckle. *$5,000*

Image courtesy of Antiquorum Auctioneers

ROLEX

- Victory, sterling silver, 17 jewel manual wind, WWII aviator's, circa 1942. *$2,250*

Watch courtesy of Derek Dier, WatchesToBuy.com

ROLEX

- Circa 1936, 9K rose gold, cushion shaped, name and date on back, sub seconds, luminous batons. *$2,200*

Watch courtesy of Heritage Auction Galleries

ROLEX

- Saturno, stainless steel, Ref. no. 3029, Arabic and baton numeral indicators, sub seconds, manual wind, with alternate stainless steel band, circa 1930s. *$800*

Watch courtesy of Skinner Inc.

ROLEX

- Oyster Perpetual, Hooded Bubble Back, in 14K rose gold and stainless steel, circa 1940. *$6,500*

Watch courtesy of Tim and Reyne Haines

(Middle)
ROLEX
- Explorer, circa 1987, Ref. 1016, stainless steel, smooth bezel, 36 mm, automatic movement. *$1,900*
Watch courtesy of Heritage Auction Galleries

(Below)
ROLEX
- Oyster, date, manual wind, white dial, silver markers, stainless steel. *$750*
Watch courtesy of Charlie Cleves - Cleves and Lonnemann Jewelers

(Top Right)
ROLEX
- Oyster Perpetual, Bubble Back, in stainless steel, circa 1945. *$1,800*
Watch courtesy of Tim and Reyne Haines

(Left)
ROLEX
- Early 3/4 size, circa 1930, stainless steel, plain bezel, oyster crown, manual wind. *$700*
Watch courtesy of Heritage Auction Galleries

(Right)
ROLEX
- Oyster, Royal, manual wind, white dial, silver markers, stainless steel. *$650*
Watch courtesy of Charlie Cleves - Cleves and Lonnemann Jewelers

(Top from Left to Right)

ROLEX

- Sterling silver, manual wind. *$800*

Watch courtesy of Leslie Hindman Auctioneers

ROLEX

- Oyster, Speedking, white dial, black enamel numerals, stainless steel. *$700*

Watch courtesy of Charlie Cleves - Cleves and Lonnemann Jewelers

(Botom Left)

ROLEX

- Military officer's hunting case in sterling silver, circa 1915. *$2,800*

Watch courtesy of Tim and Reyne Haines

(Bottom Right)

ROLEX

- Padellone, Ref. 8171, automatic, triple calendar with moon phases, circa 1950, sloped bezel, curved lugs, calendar corrector pushers on the band, gold numeral at 12 above a rose gold coronet, outer black minute marks, automatic, chronometer. Note: The ultra rare Ref. 8171 is considered to be the key watch in any serious Rolex collection. The Italian collectors gave this model the nick name "Padellone" (big pan) due to the largeness of the case and the pan shape of the back. The interior case number of 214 indicates that this was the 214th produced in the series. The model was made in a limited series of approximately 1,000 examples between 1949 and 1952, mostly in yellow gold. Examples in pink gold or in stainless steel are quite rare. *$50,000*

Watch courtesy of Heritage Auction Galleries

(Top from Left to Right)
ROLEX
- Oyster, Viceroy chronometer, automatic, stainless
  steel, pink gold bezel, Roman numerals.   *$1,600*
Watch courtesy of Charlie Cleves - Cleves and Lonnemann Jewelers

ROLEX
- Oyster, Date, stainless steel, manual
  wind, circa 1958.   *$1,200*
Watch courtesy of Heritage Auction Galleries

ROLEX
- Genève, pre-Oyster, circa 1920. Silver-cased,
  water-resistant, with enamel dial.   *$1,000*
Image courtesy of Antiquorum Auctioneers

ROLEX
- 18K white gold and diamonds,
  quartz movement.   *$3,800*
Watch courtesy of Heritage Auction Galleries

(Bottom Left)
ROLEX,
- Oyster Perpetual, date, 18K yellow gold, no
  band, white dial, Roman numerals.   *$4,000*
Watch courtesy of Charlie Cleves - Cleves and Lonnemann Jewelers

ROLEX
- Square chronograph with register, circa 1930s, Ref. 3529, stainless steel, rectangular push buttons, angled lugs, Arabic numerals, 30-minute register at 3, center sweep. Note: The Ref. 3529 is exceedingly rare. At the time of its introduction it was the smallest wrist chronograph in the world. It was produced in small numbers from 1939 to 1942. Examples in stainless steel are quite scarce. *$12,500*
Watch courtesy of Heritage Auction Galleries

(Top Middle from Left to Right)

ROLEX

- Rose gold shell, manual wind, circa 1930. *$800*

Watch courtesy of Heritage Auction Galleries

ROLEX

- Lady's, circa 1925, wire lugs, Ref. 1418, 9K yellow gold, manual wind. *$800*

Watch courtesy of Heritage Auction Galleries

ROLEX

- Circa 1920, sterling, hinged back, wire lugs, hinged front bezel, manual wind. *$800*

Watch courtesy of Heritage Auction Galleries

(Left)

ROLEX

- Lady's, circa 1950, 14K white gold, diamond bezel, manual wind, integral bracelet. *$4,400*

Watch courtesy of Heritage Auction Galleries

(Right)

ROLEX

- Lady's, circa 1970s, 14K yellow gold, diamonds, applied gold bar markers, black batons 14K yellow gold band. *$800*

Watch courtesy of Heritage Auction Galleries

(Far Right)

ROLEX

- Lady's, circa 1970, oval 14K yellow gold, manual wind, gold bracelet. *$700*

Watch courtesy of Heritage Auction Galleries

(Top from Left to Right)
ROLEX
- 18K yellow gold, manual wind, 18K yellow gold bracelet, circa 1966.   *$900*
  Watch courtesy of Heritage Auction Galleries

ROLEX
- Lady's Oyster Precision, two-tone, roulette wheel dial.   *$600*
  Watch courtesy of Phil Lucas

(Bottom Left)
ROLEX
- 14K yellow gold and diamonds, manual wind, 14K yellow gold bracelet, circa 1960.   *$1,000*
  Watch courtesy of Heritage Auction Galleries

(Botom Middle)
ROLEX
- 14K yellow gold and diamonds, 14K yellow gold bracelet, circa 1970.   *$1,000*
  Watch courtesy of Heritage Auction Galleries

(Bottom Right)
ROLEX
- 14K yellow gold with diamonds, replacement quartz movement, 14K yellow gold mesh bracelet, circa 1965.   *$1,200*
  Watch courtesy of Heritage Auction Galleries

(Left)
ROLEX
- Lady's, circa 1975, Ref. 8184, 14K yellow gold, applied gold and black enamel bar markers, black baton hands, manual wind, integral 14K band, Rolex marked box and an outer box. *$1,000*

Watch courtesy of Heritage Auction Galleries

(Below)
ROLEX
- Lady's, circa 1960s, 18K yellow gold, applied gold bar markers, manual wind, 18K gold band. *$850*

Watch courtesy of Heritage Auction Galleries

(Above)
ROLEX
- Lady's, circa 1950s, 18K gold, gold bar markers, gold batons, manual wind, 18K band. *$850*

Watch courtesy of Heritage Auction Galleries

(Left)
ROLEX
- Lady's Precision, 18K head and band, with rubies, diamonds and sapphires. *$2,000*

Watch courtesy of Charlie Cleves - Cleves and Lonnemann Jewelers

(Right)
ROLEX
- Lady's, Orchid, circa 1970s, 18K yellow gold, diamond bezel, gold and white bar markers, manual wind, 9K yellow gold band. *$1,000*

Watch courtesy of Heritage Auction Galleries

SEIKO

*S*eiko was originally founded in 1881 by Kintaro Hattori in Tokyo. However, it was not until 1924 that the first branded Seiko watches came on the market. By 1938, Seiko was producing more than a million watches a year.

Seiko has been the Official Timer of the Olympic games in Tokyo, Sapporo, Barcelona, Lillehammer and Nagano.

Seiko has had many firsts over the years. They were first to design a quartz watch, they designed the first LCD quartz watch with a six-digit display, and also the world's first intelligent analog quartz watch with alarm and timer function. In 1955 they created Japan's first self-winding watch.

In 1969, Seiko would debut the first quartz movement watch that would change the way consumers viewed wristwatches. They were more accurate than a mechanical watch, and cheaper. The quartz watch was a hit with consumers. It would also make some watch companies rethink the type of watch they produced, and it caused others to either file bankruptcy or close their doors for good.

Seiko is still in business today producing chronographs and perpetual-calendar watches.

SEIKO
- **Lordmatic, 39mm, stainless steel, 25 jewel automatic.** *$250*
  Watch courtesy of Derek Dier, WatchesToBuy.com

TIFFANY & CO.

*T*iffany & Co. was founded in 1837 by Charles Lewis Tiffany and Charles B. Young. It was originally called Tiffany & Young. The company was known for offering the finest luxury goods in the country. By 1853, Tiffany had gained control of the company and the name was changed to Tiffany & Co.

Over the years, Tiffany & Co. has been asked to produce an array of historical items. For the inauguration of Abraham Lincoln, Tiffany designed a special pitcher. They were also asked to produce crockery for the White House featuring the 50 birds of America. In 1855, Tiffany & Co. redesigned the seal for the United States of America.

Tiffany & Co. not only designs watches, but also fine silver, jewelry and other luxury goods. In 1870, its watch factory in Switzerland was one of the largest in the region.

Tiffany & Co. is still in business today. All of their watches come with a 5-year warranty.

Charles Lewis Tiffany

(Far Left)
TIFFANY & CO.
- 14K yellow gold, Concord movement, circa 1930. *$800*
  Watch courtesy of Heritage Auction Galleries

(Top Left)
TIFFANY & CO.
- Concord, 14K yellow gold, sub second, manual wind, circa 1950s. *$550*
  Watch courtesy of Phil Lucas

(Bottom Left)
TIFFANY & CO.
- Art Deco lady's, platinum, silver-tone dial with Arabic numeral indicators. *$700*
  Watch courtesy of Skinner Inc.

(Top from Left to Right)
TIFFANY & CO.
- Calendar by Movado, circa 1940s, 14K yellow gold, beveled lugs, two-tone dial, Arabic numerals and markers, subsidiary seconds, case and movement signed Movado, dial signed Tiffany & Co.   *$1,400*
Watch courtesy of Heritage Auction Galleries

TIFFANY & CO
- 14K yellow gold, quartz movement.   *$775*
Watch courtesy of Leslie Hindman Auctioneers

TIFFANY & CO.
- 14K yellow gold, quartz movement.   *$900*
Watch courtesy of Leslie Hindman Auctioneers

(Bottom Right)
TIFFANY & CO.
- Platinum, manual wind.   *$3,500*
Watch courtesy of Heritage Auction Galleries

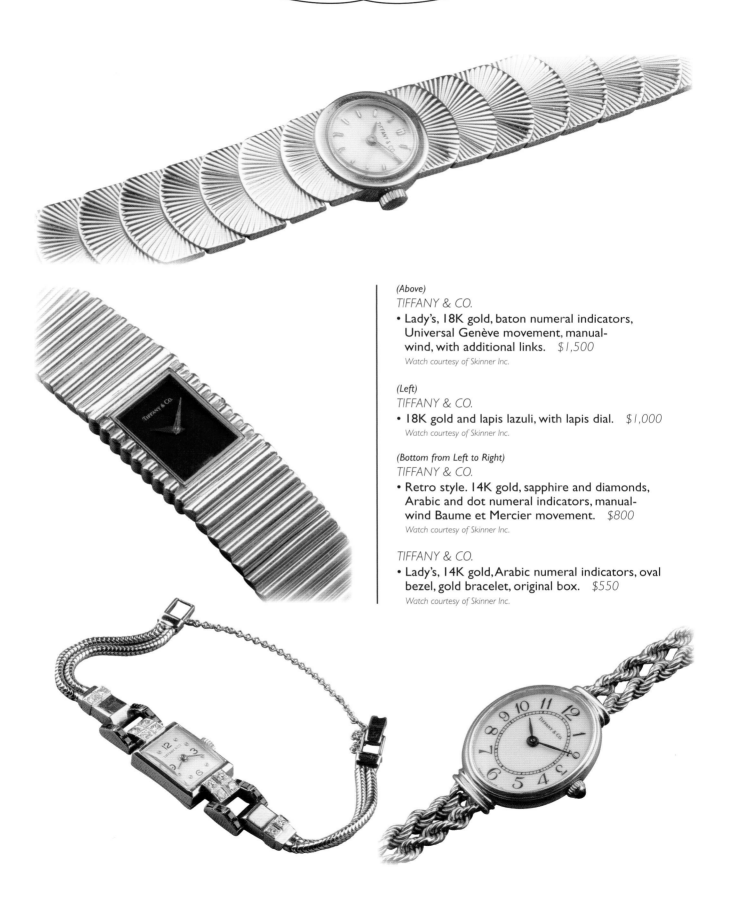

(Above)
TIFFANY & CO.
- Lady's, 18K gold, baton numeral indicators, Universal Genève movement, manual-wind, with additional links.   *$1,500*

Watch courtesy of Skinner Inc.

(Left)
TIFFANY & CO.
- 18K gold and lapis lazuli, with lapis dial.   *$1,000*

Watch courtesy of Skinner Inc.

(Bottom from Left to Right)
TIFFANY & CO.
- Retro style. 14K gold, sapphire and diamonds, Arabic and dot numeral indicators, manual-wind Baume et Mercier movement.   *$800*

Watch courtesy of Skinner Inc.

TIFFANY & CO.
- Lady's, 14K gold, Arabic numeral indicators, oval bezel, gold bracelet, original box.   *$550*

Watch courtesy of Skinner Inc.

TISSOT

T̲issot was established in 1853. The founders were Charles-Felicien Tissot and his son, Charles-Emile Tissot. The firm was located in Le Lode, Switzerland.

Tissot has created many firsts in the watch world. They created the first antimagnetic watch, and also were the first to produce the plastic watch.

Tissot watches have been used in important sporting events such as downhill skiing in Switzerland in 1938, and also the Davis Cup in 1957. Tissot was also recognized as the authorized timekeeper for road biking, circuit racing, cycling and ice hockey events.

(Above)
MATHEY-TISSOT
- 14K white gold and diamonds, circa 1950.   *$775*

Watch courtesy of Heritage Auction Galleries

(Left)
MATHEY-TISSOT
- 18K yellow gold, $20 gold coin, manual wind.   *$2,000*

Watch courtesy of Heritage Auction Galleries

(Left)
MATHEY-TISSOT
- Circa 1970, 14K yellow gold, diamond bezel, gold and black bar markers, manual wind, 14K band.   *$800*
Watch courtesy of Heritage Auction Galleries

(Right)
MATHEY-TISSOT
- Masonic, circa 1950s, sterling silver, gold markers and Masonic symbols, manual wind.   *$1,000*
Watch courtesy of Heritage Auction Galleries

(Left)
MATHEY-TISSOT
- Circa 1975, $20 1904 Liberty coin as 22k gold outer case, recessed 18K hinged inner case, coin edge (second view closed).   *$1,600*
Watch courtesy of Heritage Auction Galleries

(Left)
MATHEY-TISSOT
- Manual wind, silver dial, sub second, gold bar markers, 14K yellow gold. *$300*
  Watch courtesy of Charlie Cleves - Cleves and Lonnemann Jewelers

(Top Right)
MATHEY-TISSOT
- Circa 1960s, 18K yellow gold, date at 3, gold and black batons, center seconds, manual wind. *$275*
  Watch courtesy of Heritage Auction Galleries

(Bottom Middle)
TISSOT
- Circa 1960, 14K yellow gold, date at 3, black markers, black batons, gold sweep hand, manual wind. *$150*
  Watch courtesy of Heritage Auction Galleries

(Bottom Right)
TISSOT
- Visodate circa 1960s, 14K pink gold, tapered lugs, applied gold markers, date at 3, manual wind. *$225*
  Watch courtesy of Heritage Auction Galleries

TUDOR

*T*he Tudor brand emerged on the market in 1946. It was launched by Rolex founder, Hans Wilsdorf. The name "Tudor" was chosen to honor the Tudor period of England.

Tudor watches were signed on the dial "Tudor" and with the Tudor Rose, which was the heraldic emblem of England. In the 1960s, Tudor replaced the Rose with a shield.

One of the key differences in the Tudor brand was the movement. Tudor was using movements supplied by Ebauches SA instead of Rolex movements.

Many of the Tudor watches were modeled after Rolex designs. Their sizes were the same, and often the model names were the same. (i.e. Tudor Submariner). However, the Tudor line was primarily produced in stainless steel, unlike the two-toned and solid gold options offered by Rolex.

In the 1960s, the French Navy began purchasing Tudor Submariners for their divers. The U.S. Navy and the Navy Seals later followed suit.

In 1997, golf professional Tiger Woods became the face of Tudor. The Tiger Woods Tudor Chronograph was offered with an array of exotic dials.

Still in production today, Tudor watches are sold in Asia, Canada, Europe and Latin America.

(Above)
TUDOR
• Oyster Perpetual, stainless steel, manual wind, circa 1958.   *$2,000*
Watch courtesy of Heritage Auction Galleries

(Left)
TUDOR
• Advisor, alarm, stainless steel.   *$1,650*
Watch courtesy of Phil Lucas

TUDOR
- Oyster Prince, self-wind, in stainless steel, Deco dial, circa 1940.   *$700*

Watch courtesy of Tim and Reyne Haines

TUDOR
- Stainless steel, gilt dial, 34.5mm, automatic, 1960s.   *$1,150*

Watch courtesy of Derek Dier, WatchesToBuy.com

TUDOR
- "Tuxedo dial," 17 jewel, automatic, stainless steel, circa 1956.   *$1,500*

Watch courtesy of Derek Dier, WatchesToBuy.com

TUDOR
- Prince Oysterdate, automatic, gold plated, 34mm, 1970s.   *$995*

Watch courtesy of Derek Dier, WatchesToBuy.com

TUDOR
- Lady's, Oysterdate, 23mm, gold and steel, 21 jewel automatic.   *$795*

Watch courtesy of Derek Dier, WatchesToBuy.com

TUDOR
- Tuxedo, 17 jewel automatic, 1960s.   *$1,650*

Watch courtesy of Derek Dier, WatchesToBuy.com

(Top from Left to Right)
TUDOR
- Automatic, 34.5mm, stainless steel, 1950s. *$1,250*

Watch courtesy of Derek Dier, WatchesToBuy.com

TUDOR
- Oyster, Regent, 31.5mm, gold plated, 17 jewel manual wind, circa 1950s. *$250*

Watch courtesy of Derek Dier, WatchesToBuy.com

TUDOR
- Oyster, Air-Lion, stainless steel, 17 jewel manual wind, 32mm, 1950s. *$975*

Watch courtesy of Derek Dier, WatchesToBuy.com

(Bottom Left)
TUDOR
- Oyster, 21 jewel, stainless steel, smooth bezel. *$700*

Watch courtesy of Phil Lucas

TUDOR
- Stainless steel, 35mm, 17 jewel manual wind, 1947. *$900*

Watch courtesy of Derek Dier, WatchesToBuy.com

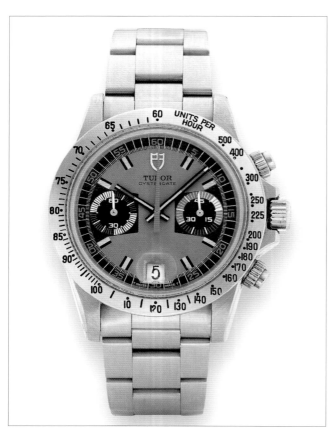

TUDOR
- Oyster-Date, automatic, Ref. 79160, case made by Rolex, 1980. Self-winding, water resistant to 100 meters, stainless steel with round-button chronograph, registers, tachometer, date and a stainless steel Tudor Oyster bracelet.   *$2,500*

Image courtesy of Antiquorum Auctioneers

TUDOR
- Oyster Prince, day/date Rotor, Ref. 7017/0, case made by Rolex, 1960s. Center seconds, self-winding, water-resistant to 100 meters, stainless steel with a stainless steel link bracelet.   *$750*

Image courtesy of Antiquorum Auctioneers

TUDOR
- Oyster, Ref. 7159/0, case made by Rolex, 1972. Water-resistant, stainless steel with date, round-button chronograph, register, tachometer and a stainless steel Rolex Oyster bracelet.   *$9,000*

Image courtesy of Antiquorum Auctioneers

TUDOR
- Advisor, stainless steel, alarm, 17 jewel manual wind, 1970s.   *$2,695*

Watch courtesy of Derek Dier, WatchesToBuy.com

TUDOR
- Submariner, Ref. 7528, stainless steel, 17 jewel, automatic, circa 1968.   *$3,500*

Watch courtesy of Derek Dier, WatchesToBuy.com

ULYSSE NARDIN

$\mathcal{U}$ lysse Nardin, named after its founder, was established in 1846 in Le Locle, Switzerland. The firm was best known for its marine chronometers.

Nardin was an accomplished watchmaker who had studied horology under his father, Leonard-Frederic Nardin, and other recognized watchmakers such as Frederic William Dubois and Louis Jean Richard-dit-Bressel.

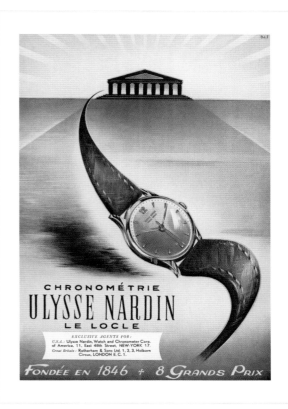

ULYSEE NARDIN
- "1846" marine chronometer, circa 2000, stainless steel, No. 1564, back inscribed with Nardin gold medal dates and world locations, coin edge on the bezel, screw-down crown, automatic movement.   *$3,300*

Watch courtesy of Heritage Auction Galleries

ULYSSE NARDIN
- Locle & Genève, circa 1980. Tonneau-shaped 18K yellow gold with triple date and moon phases. Accompanied by a fitted box.   *$2,500*

Image courtesy of Antiquorum Auctioneers

ULYSSE NARDIN
- "High-beat" chronometer, 36mm, stainless steel, automatic, circa 1975.   *$2,000*

Watch courtesy of Derek Dier, WatchesToBuy.com

UNIVERSAL GENÈVE

*U*niversal Genève was first founded under the name Universal Watch in 1894 by watchmakers Numa-Emile Descombes, and Ulysse Georges Perret. Together, they registered the company name for the production of dials, watch movements, pocket-watch domes and cases, and watch boxes. At the same time, they also patented a 24-hour indication watch.

In 1897, co-founder Descombes died and all patents were transferred to Perret and Louis-Edouard Berthoud.

The Universal Watch brand was gaining popularity in Europe and in America. The company was rapidly expanding. They relocated their headquarters to Geneva in 1919. By 1925, Universal had designed their first self-winding watch called the "Auto Rem."

In 1933, founder Perret died. His son, Raoul, took over the company and the name was changed to Universal Watch Co. Ltd. Genève in 1934. Raoul then registered the name "Universal Genève" in 1937 and changed the brand logo.

The management of Universal Genève taken at Les Ponts-de-Martel, Switzerland, in 1941.

(Far Left)
UNIVERSAL GENÈVE
- Polerouter, gold capped, 34.5mm, 28 jewel automatic. *$900*

Watch courtesy of Derek Dier, WatchesToBuy.com

(Left)
UNIVERSAL GENÈVE
- Polerouter, gold capped, 34.5mm, 28 jewel automatic. *$900*

Watch courtesy of Derek Dier, WatchesToBuy.com

(Middle)
UNIVERSAL GENÈVE
- Polerouter, automatic, 1960s. Large, center seconds, self-winding, water-resistant, stainless steel. *$4,000*
  Image courtesy of Antiquorum Auctioneers

(Top Right)
UNIVERSAL GENÈVE
- Polerouter, automatic, circa 1960, 14K yellow gold, straight lugs, No. 45838, 36 mm diameter. *$700*
  Watch courtesy of Heritage Auction Galleries

(Bottom Right)
UNIVERSAL GENÈVE
- Automatic, stainless steel, circa 1950s. *$175*
  Watch courtesy of Chris Miller

Despite the effects of the Great Depression, Universal Genève found success with two of their designs, "Compax" and "Compur." In fact, the watch lines were so popular the factory could not keep up with the demand.

In 1954, a new chronograph was introduced, the "Polerouter" (initially named Polarouter). The watch was used by the SAS during their polar flights.

The "Polerouter" was the thinnest automatic movement of its time. Developing thin, automatic movements became a standard for Universal Genève. In 1966, the company introduced the "Golden Shadow," just 2.5mm in thickness.

Universal Genève partnered with other watch companies over the years to create new and inventive products. In 1962 they worked with Movado to create an electric watch. In 1968 they worked with the American watchmaker, Bulova, to create an electronic watch with a "Tuning Unisonic" system.

Numerous watch companies found themselves in desperate times with the arrival of the Japanese quartz watch. Universal, however, was able to design the thinnest analog quartz watch movement at the time in 1975, which helped prevent their demise.

Universal had numerous "recognized" clients. Artist Jean Cocteau was so impressed by their designs, he composed the dedication, "Les temps lui-meme regarde l'heure á la montre Universal," which Universal put on the dials of the tourbillion models. Gen. Juan Peron and Harry Truman were also fans of Universal Genève.

Universal Genève is currently owned by Stelux Holding Group, Hong Kong.

UNIVERSAL GENÈVE

- Circa 1930, 18K rose gold, claw lugs, silver dial with sub seconds, rose gold markers and numerals, rose gold Dauphine hands, manual wind, in a red Universal box Genève.   *$750*

Watch courtesy of Heritage Auction Galleries

UNIVERSAL GENÈVE

- Manual wind, square dial, sub second, 18K yellow gold.   *$500*

Watch courtesy of Charlie Cleves - Cleves and Lonnemann Jewelers

UNIVERSAL GENÈVE

- Circa 1950s, 18K rose gold, rose gold dauphine hands, center sweep hand, automatic.   *$1,000*

Watch courtesy of Heritage Auction Galleries

UNIVERSAL GENÈVE
- Uni-Compax doctor's chronograph, circa 1940s, 18K rose gold, rectangular pushers, gold markers, 45-minute register, constant seconds at 9, manual wind. *$1,400*

Watch courtesy of Heritage Auction Galleries

UNIVERSAL GENÈVE
- Stainless steel, chronograph, manual wind. *$650*

Watch courtesy of Leslie Hindman Auctioneers

UNIVERSAL GENÈVE
- Calendar, circa 1990, skeleton back with sapphire crystal, 18K gold, Ref. 1511.11.664, No. 97, beaded edge to front and back, coin edge to the rim, teardrop lugs, automatic movement. *$1,600*

Watch courtesy of Heritage Auction Galleries

UNIVERSAL GENÈVE
- Automatic, triple calendar with moon phase, stainless and 18K, circa 1980s. *$2,500*

Watch courtesy of Chris Miller

UNIVERSAL GENÈVE
- Three-register chronograph, automatic, circa 1980s. *$1,700*

Watch courtesy of Chris Miller

VACHERON CONSTANTIN

*T*he story of Vacheron & Constantin begins in 1755 in Geneva. They are the oldest watch manufacturer in the world with an uninterrupted history. The company was founded by Jean-Marc Vacheron, a young talented watchmaker.

In 1770, Vacheron created his first complicated movement. In 1779, he was making the first engine-turned dials.

In 1785, the company was taken over by Vacheron's son, Abraham. In 1810, the grandson of the founder, Jaques-Barthèlemy, took over the business.

Jacques-Barthèlemy began exporting watches to France and Italy. He wanted to expand the business further, but realized he could not do this alone. In 1819, François Constantin was brought in as Vacheron's associate to take the company to the next level. It was at this time the company began using the name "Vacheron & Constantin."

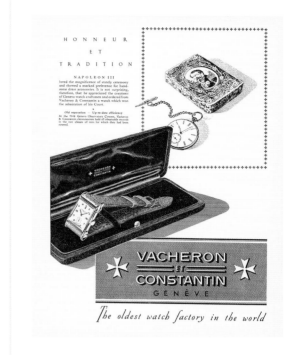

Before long, Vacheron & Constantin hired Georges-Auguste Leschot, an inventor. His designs were wildly successful. He was the first person to standardize movements into calibers. In 1844 he was awarded a gold medal at the Arts Society of Geneva for his pantographic tool. This device allowed a watchmaker to engrave watch parts and dials.

In 1854, François Constantin died, and in 1863, Jaques-Barthèlemy died. The company was managed over the next several years by numerous heirs and reorganized in 1887. Also that year, the company was awarded a gold medal at the Swiss National Exhibition in Geneva.

Vacheron & Constantin opened their first shop in Geneva in 1906. This store is still open today.

One of the most expensive watches on the market today is the "Kallista" by Vacheron & Constantin. It was created in 1979, and originally sold for $5 million. Today the watch is valued around $11 million. The watch offers more than 100 emerald-cut diamonds, and took 6,000 hours to create.

Vacheron & Constantin dropped the "&" from their name in 1979. They are still in operation today, owned by the Richemont Group. They produce approximately 20,000 watches a year, and are headquartered in Plan-les-Ouates, Geneva.

VACHERON CONSTANTIN
- Platinum, "Gerard Mercator 1594" - 1994, circa 1994.   *$18,500*

Watch courtesy of Heritage Auction Galleries

(Above)

VACHERON & CONSTANTIN
- Fancy lugs, No. 465173, case No. 304922, 1940s, 18K yellow gold.   *$6,500*

  Image courtesy of Antiquorum Auctioneers

(Top Right)

VACHERON & CONSTANTIN
- 18K yellow gold, sub second, manual wind, circa 1960s.   *$4,500*

  Watch courtesy of James F. Dicke II

(Bottom Right)

VACHERON & CONSTANTIN
- 14K yellow gold, manual wind.   *$2,500*

  Watch courtesy of Leslie Hindman Auctioneers

(Bottom Far Right)

VACHERON & CONSTANTIN
- Circa 1960s, 18K yellow gold, angled lugs, sub seconds, applied bar markers, manual wind.   *$1,750*

  Watch courtesy of Heritage Auction Galleries

(Top from Left to Right)
VACHERON CONSTANTIN
- Classique Patrimony, modern, 18K white gold, sapphire crystals, manual wind. *$5,975*

Watch courtesy of Heritage Auction Galleries

VACHERON & CONSTANTIN
- No. 457501, case No. 290218, Ref. 4240, 1946, 18K yellow gold with triple calendar and claw lugs. Accompanied by period blank Vacheron Constantin certificate and display stand. *$10,000*

Image courtesy of Antiquorum Auctioneers

(Bottom Left)
VACHERON & CONSTANTIN
- Chronograph, No. 466730, case No. 328772, Ref. 4072, 1952, 18K pink gold with square-button chronograph, register, telemeter and tachometer. *$25,000*

Image courtesy of Antiquorum Auctioneers

(Bottom Middle)
VACHERON & CONSTANTIN
- Platinum and diamonds, manual wind, circa 1918. *$3,000*

Watch courtesy of Heritage Auction Galleries

(Bottom Right)
VACHERON & CONSTANTIN
- 18K yellow gold, teardrop lugs, manual wind, circa 1945. *$2,200*

Watch courtesy of Heritage Auction Galleries

VACHERON & CONSTANTIN
- No. 605939, case No. 429124, Ref. 7403, 1960s. Thin, tonneau-shaped, 18K yellow gold. *$1,500*
  Image courtesy of Antiquorum Auctioneers

VACHERON CONSTANTIN
- Automatic, circa 1990, 18K white gold, water resistant, ultra thin. *$5,300*
  Watch courtesy of Heritage Auction Galleries

VACHERON CONSTANTIN FOR LECOULTRE
- "Mystery Dial," diamond numbers and hands, 14K white gold. *$3,000*
  Watch courtesy of Charlie Cleves - Cleves and Lonnemann Jewelers

VACHERON & CONSTANTIN
- 18K yellow gold, sweep second. *$2,500*
  Watch courtesy of Leslie Hindman Auctioneers

VACHERON & CONSTANTIN
- Center seconds, circa 1960, 18K, screw back, curved lugs, recessed crown, Ref. 6308, No. 366147. *$2,800*
  Watch courtesy of Heritage Auction Galleries

(Top from Left to Right)

VACHERON & CONSTANTIN

- Circa 1945, 18K yellow gold, stepped lugs, applied gold numerals, sub seconds.   *$2,500*

Watch courtesy of Heritage Auction Galleries

VACHERON & CONSTANTIN

- Circa 1938, 18K rose gold, teardrop lugs, rose gold Roman numerals, sub seconds, manual wind.   *$2,500*

Watch courtesy of Heritage Auction Galleries

(Bottom Left)

VACHERON & CONSTANTIN

- Platinum, manual wind, circa 1920.   *$3,500*

Watch courtesy of Heritage Auction Galleries

(Bottom Middle)

VACHERON & CONSTANTIN

- Lady's, circa 1965, 18K, cushion shape, engraved bezel, manual wind.   *$700*

Watch courtesy of Heritage Auction Galleries

(Bottom Right)

VACHERON & CONSTANTIN

- 18K yellow gold, manual wind.   *$750*

Watch courtesy of Heritage Auction Galleries

VAN CLEEF & ARPELS

*V*an Cleef & Arpels was established in 1906 by Alfred Van Cleef and his new wife, Estelle, along with her brother, Charles Arpels. The firm was opened as a jewelry design house in Paris. Eventually the company added Estelle's other brothers, Julian and Louis, to the firm.

Van Cleef & Arpels was always recognized for their sophisticated style of jewelry. They offered their clients nothing but the best, using diamonds, emeralds, rubies and sapphires.

It wasn't until 1920 that the firm added watches to its line of luxury goods.

Van Cleef & Arpels has more than 50 boutiques around the world.

VAN CLEEF & ARPELS
- **18K yellow gold and diamond, circa 1940s.** *$6,000*
Watch courtesy of Leslie Hindman Auctioneers

VULCAIN

*M*aurice Ditisheim Fabrique Vulcain launched a line of wristwatches bearing the name "Vulcain" in 1894. However, this was not the first production for Ditisheim. He had been producing pocket watches in La Chaux-de-Fonds, Switzerland, since 1858.

The year 1947 proved to be the most important year for Vulcain when the "Cricket" was introduced. The Cricket was the company's first wrist alarm watch. It was highly successful and eventually went on to be more than just an alarm. In the 1950s there was the Cricket Calendar, which offered a date window. The 1960s saw the Cricket Nautical, which was watertight to a depth of 300 meters.

In the 1980s, after the introduction of the quartz watch, Vulcain all but disappeared. Vulcain continued to produce watches for a few brands, such as Revue Thommen. In the late 1990s, the firm was sold. In 2001 the brand name Vulcain and the Cricket caliber were acquired by Production et Marketing Horologer (PMH).

PMH moved the firm from La Chaux-de-Fonds to Le Locle, Switzerland. PMH began producing Vulcain watches again in 2002.

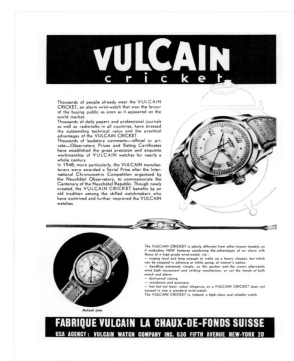

VULCAIN
- **Stainless steel, chronograph, manual wind.** *$335*
Watch courtesy of Leslie

WAKMANN

The Wakmann Watch Co. was founded in New York. They were importers of high-quality wristwatches to North America.

The company was eventually purchased by Breitling, allowing the firm to ship their movements to the U.S. and have them set and sold in cases.

Some Breitling watches carry Wakmann-marked movements. Some Wakmann watches have Breitling movements. Wakmann also bought movements from Landeron, Lemania and Valjoux. Some are fine quality; some were cheaply made.

WAKMANN
- **Stainless steel triple-date chronograph, 37mm, Valjoux 723, manual wind, 1960s.** *$1,695*

Watch courtesy of Derek Dier, WatchesToBuy.com

WALTHAM

The American Waltham Watch Co. was founded in Massachusetts in 1850. They were considered one of the largest watch manufacturers of the 19th century.

The company was founded by three gentlemen, Mr. Davis, Mr. Dension and Mr. Howard. They each felt quality watches could be made without the need of expensive materials often used by other watchmakers. Unfortunately, their concept of inexpensive materials failed and the company was under extreme financial stress.

The company changed names numerous times over the years. Initially, their watch brand was "American Horology Company." By 1852, the company was branding watches with the name "The Warren Manufacturing Company." The first 110 watches produced had various names on the dial. The first 17 were given to company officials and executives. Watches 18 - 110 were engraved with the name "Warren Boston." The next 800 watches were signed "Samuel Curtis" and a few were marked "Fellows and Schel." In 1853, the company name was changed again to Boston Watch Co.

The Boston Watch Co. struggled to keep afloat, and in 1857 was auctioned to the highest bidder, Royal E. Robbins. The company would change names yet again and would be known as Appleton, Tracey & Co. In 1859, the company would merge with the Waltham Improvement Co. to form the American Waltham Watch Co. This firm went out of business in 1957.

It is said that the Waltham Watch Co. produced about 40 million watches, clocks, speedometers, compasses, time fuses and other instruments between 1850 and 1957.

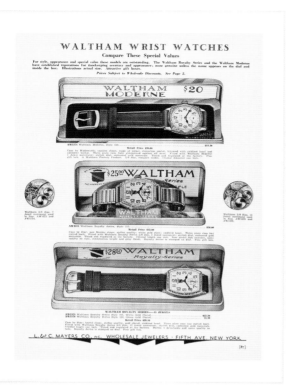

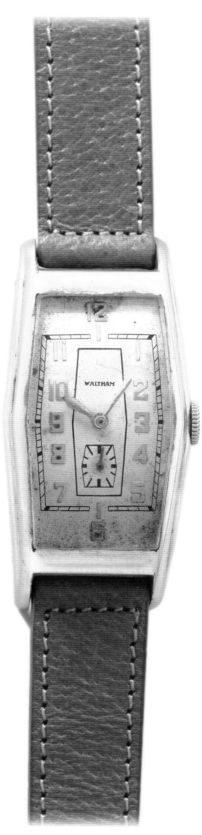

(Bottom Far Left)
WALTHAM
• Masonic, circa 1960s, gold-plated bezel, stainless back, upper circular lug with Masonic compass and rule, center sweep, with motto, "Love your fellow man, lend him a helping hand", manual wind. *$500*

Watch courtesy of Heritage Auction Galleries

(Left)
WALTHAM
• Long case, manual wind, gold applied numerals, yellow gold filled, circa 1930s, 48mm. *$500*

Watch courtesy of Charlie Cleves - Cleves and Lonnemann Jewelers

WITTNAUER

The Wittnauer Watch Co. has an interesting history. In 1872, a 16-year-old Swiss immigrant arrived New York City. Albert Wittnauer had already learned how to produce high-quality watches and had worked for his brother-in-law, J. Eugene Robert, exporting fine Swiss watches. Wittnauer decided there was a need for watches with high durability and function in America. His designs were an instant hit with his brother-in-law's clients.

In 1890, the company was established under the name A. Wittnauer Co. Employing only the top-of-the-line watchmakers, Wittnauer quickly became known in the niche market of timepieces for exploration. A noted horologist is quoted as saying, "No one company has been more involved in the design and production of so many different types of navigational timepieces and been involved in so many history-making expeditions …"

Wittnauer is still in business today as part of the Bulova Watch Co.

WITTNAUER
- Lady's, 14K pink gold, manual wind with diamonds and rubies. *$250*

Watch courtesy of Charlie Cleves - Cleves and Lonnemann Jewelers

WITTNAUER
- Manual wind, white dial, gold numerals,. 14K yellow gold. *$250*

Watch courtesy of Charlie Cleves - Cleves and Lonnemann Jewelers

WITTNAUER
- Valjoux 72 chronograph, manual wind, 36mm, stainless steel. *$1,700*

Watch courtesy of Derek Dier, WatchesToBuy.com

WITTNAUER
- Genève Professional, stainless steel, 36mm, Landeron 248 manual wind, 1960s. *$995*

Watch courtesy of Derek Dier, WatchesToBuy.com

WITTNAUER
- Gold filled, day/date, 31.5mm, manual wind, 1950s. *$450*

Watch courtesy of Derek Dier, WatchesToBuy.com

WITTNAUER
- Lady's, manual wind, 10K white gold and diamonds. *$225*

Watch courtesy of Charlie Cleves - Cleves and Lonnemann Jewelers

WITTNAUER
- Electro Chron, stainless steel, 35mm, 1960s. *$900*

Watch courtesy of Derek Dier, WatchesToBuy.com

WITTNAUER
- Stainless steel, automatic, sweep second, circa 1960. *$100*

Watch courtesy of Leslie Hindman Auctioneers

ZENITH

The first Zenith-brand wristwatches arrived on the market in 1920. The factory had produced fob watches since the 1870s. Prior to making watches, founded George Favre-Jacot was a clock maker.

In 1954, Zenith won the Neuchatel Observatory prize for their chronometer wristwatches. In 1969, the line "El Primero" debuted. This was the first chronograph in the world equipped with a winding crown with a central rotor.

In 1971, the Zenith Radio Corp. took a majority stake in the Mondia-Zenith-Movado Group, which in 1984 was taken over by the North American Watch Co. In 2000, Zenith was taken over by the L.V.M.H. group.

(Far Left)
ZENITH
- 18K yellow gold, 18K yellow gold mesh bracelet, circa 1950. *$2,100*
Watch courtesy of Heritage Auction Galleries

(Left Top to Bottom)
ZENITH
- Movement No.2001129, 1930s. Sterling silver cushion-cased, with enamel dial and red 12. *$500*
Image courtesy of Antiquorum Auctioneers

ZENITH
- Ref. 848A752, 1960s, 18K yellow gold with square-button chronograph, register and tachometer. *$2,000*
Image courtesy of Antiquorum Auctioneers

ZODIAC

ZODIAC
- 40mm, chronograph, Valjoux 7734, manual wind, 1970s. *$450*

Watch courtesy of Derek Dier, WatchesToBuy.com

*T*he Zodiac Watch Co. was founded in 1882 in Le Locle, Switzerland, by Ariste Calame. Calame's ambitions were to create a watch like no other. Zodiac watches were known for their quality and innovation. A few firsts by Zodiac were the first Swiss-designed automatic sports watch in 1930; the first professional sports and divers watch in 1953; the first Swiss analog quartz watch in 1970; and the patent of a shock resistant case in 1974.

Zodiac timepieces have won several awards over the years. In 1965 they won a prize at the Montres et Bijoux Exhibition in Geneva. In 1967 they won first prize at the World's Fair in Montreal.

Zodiac is still manufacturing fine timepieces today.

ZODIAC
- Stainless steel, manual wind. *$100*

Watch courtesy of Leslie Hindman Auctioneers

ZODIAC
- Sea Wolf, triple date moon phase, 34.5mm, 17 jewel automatic. *$1,350*

Watch courtesy of Derek Dier, WatchesToBuy.com

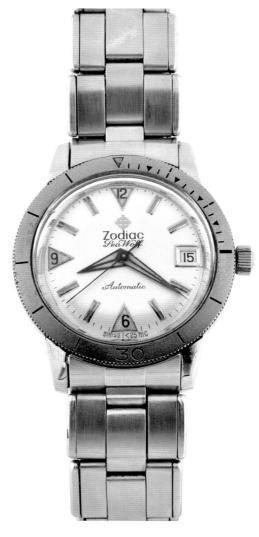

(Top from Left to Right)
ZODIAC
• Sea Wolf, 17 jewel, automatic
  with uncommon bezel. *$950*
  Watch courtesy of Derek Dier, WatchesToBuy.com

ZODIAC
• Sea Wolf, diver's, 35.5mm, stainless
  steel, 17 jewel automatic. *$795*
  Watch courtesy of Derek Dier, WatchesToBuy.com

(Bottom from Left to Right)
ZODIAC
• Astrographic SST, 36mm, stainless
  steel, 21 jewel. *$550*
  Watch courtesy of Derek Dier, WatchesToBuy.com

ZODIAC
• Stainless steel, manual wind. *$350*
  Watch courtesy of Leslie Hindman Auctioneers

OTHER MAKERS

BRADLEY
- Mickey Mouse, 32mm, stainless steel, circa 1970. *$250*

Watch courtesy of Derek Dier, WatchesToBuy.com

CERTINA
- 17 jewel automatic, 29.5mm, gold filled. *$275*

Watch courtesy of Derek Dier, WatchesToBuy.com

BULGARI
- 18K yellow gold, gold integral bracelet, quartz movement. *$4,000*

Watch courtesy of Heritage Auction Galleries

ENICAR
- Sherpa-Graph, 40mm, stainless steel, Valjoux 72 movement, manual wind. *$2,495*

Watch courtesy of Derek Dier, WatchesToBuy.com

ESKA DIGITAL
- Direct read, 29mm, chromium case, manual wind, 1930s. *$995*

Watch courtesy of Derek Dier, WatchesToBuy.com

FRANCK MULLER
- "Crazy Hours," circa 2000, 18K rose gold, tonneau case, sapphire crystal, back marked "Master of Complications, No. 51,7851, Crazy Hours". *$13,145*

Watch courtesy of Heritage Auction Galleries

FREY
- Chronograph, 36.5mm, chromium, Valjoux 22, manual wind, 1940s. *$800*

Watch courtesy of Derek Dier, WatchesToBuy.com

HELIOS
- WWII, 15 jewel manual wind, 32mm, chromium plated. *$650*

Watch courtesy of Derek Dier, WatchesToBuy.com

GILBERT
- James Bond 007 novelty, 60mm, plastic and metal, 1960s. *$900*

Watch courtesy of Derek Dier, WatchesToBuy.com

INGERSOLL
- Manual wind, white dial, gold numerals, yellow gold plated. *$40*

Watch courtesy of Tim and Reyne Haines

JACCARD
- 14K yellow gold, manual wind, circa 1940s. *$150*

Watch courtesy of Chris Miller

HOVERTA
- Automatic, diver's, 17 jewel, 42mm, circa 1975. *$650*

Watch courtesy of Derek Dier, WatchesToBuy.com

LEAD
- Swiss made, 14K and sapphire, 16mm, 15 jewel manual wind, 1930s. *$600*

Watch courtesy of Derek Dier, WatchesToBuy.com

LE JOUR
- Chronograph, 35mm, gold plated, Valjoux 7733, manual wind. *$700*

Watch courtesy of Derek Dier, WatchesToBuy.com

LORD ELCO
- 32.5mm, gold filled, 17 jewel manual wind. *$250*

Watch courtesy of Derek Dier, WatchesToBuy.com

LEXON
- Mangraf Super, 49mm, Valjoux 7734, manual wind, stainless steel chronograph. *$795*

Watch courtesy of Derek Dier, WatchesToBuy.com

LOYAL
- Stainless steel, waterproof, 17 jewel, screwed back, 37mm, 1940. *$675*

Watch courtesy of Derek Dier, WatchesToBuy.com

LUCIEN PICCARD
- Lady's, circa 1965, 14K yellow gold, pearls, 18 mm, two piece, No. C 2195, manual wind. *$700*

Watch courtesy of Heritage Auction Galleries

LUCIEN PICCARD
- Seashark, 14K yellow gold. *$475*
Watch courtesy of Leslie Hindman Auctioneers

LUCIEN PICCARD
- Seashark, circa 1960s, 14K yellow gold, black dial, diamond and bar markers, automatic. *$175*
Watch courtesy of Heritage Auction Galleries

MEDANA
- Stainless steel, 32mm, 17 jewel, 1940s. *$300*
Watch courtesy of Derek Dier, WatchesToBuy.com

LUCIEN PICCARD
- 14K yellow gold with diamonds, quartz movement, 14K yellow gold bracelet. *$500*
Watch courtesy of Heritage Auction Galleries

LUCIEN PICCARD
- 14K white gold, manual wind, 14K white gold bracelet, circa 1960. *$400*
Watch courtesy of Heritage Auction Galleries

MIMO
- Stainless steel, 35mm, 17 jewel, WWII. *$950*
Watch courtesy of Derek Dier, WatchesToBuy.com

NIVADA
- 1,000 ft. diver's, 40mm, 21 jewel, 1970. *$1,500*

Watch courtesy of Derek Dier, WatchesToBuy.com

OLMA
- 18K rose gold, 19 jewel manual wind, 1940s. *$700*

Watch courtesy of Derek Dier, WatchesToBuy.com

ORATOR
- Lady's cocktail, 16mm, 18K rose gold, 17 jewel manual wind, 1950s. *$500*

Watch courtesy of Derek Dier, WatchesToBuy.com

PIQUETTE
- 14K gold, 34mm, 17 jewel manual wind. *$675*

Watch courtesy of Derek Dier, WatchesToBuy.com

NORMANDIE
- Manual wind, silver dial, sub second, black numerals, fancy lugs. *$300*

Watch courtesy of Charlie Cleves - Cleves and Lonnemann Jewelers

REVUE
- Sport, WWII German military, 32mm, manual wind. *$850*

Watch courtesy of Derek Dier, WatchesToBuy.com

ROYCE
• Dual time, 30mm,
stainless steel, 17 jewel
manual wind. *$900*
*Watch courtesy of Derek
Dier, WatchesToBuy.com*

ROYCE
• Lady's, hexagonal, 27mm,
stainless steel, 17 jewel
manual wind. *$300*
*Watch courtesy of Derek
Dier, WatchesToBuy.com*

RADO
• Starliner, 25 jewel automatic, stainless steel, 38mm. *$275*
Watch courtesy of Derek Dier, WatchesToBuy.com

ROYCE
• Professional Marine, diver's, 46mm, anodized
steel, automatic, 1970s. *$2,000*
Watch courtesy of Derek Dier, WatchesToBuy.com

ROYCE
• Lady's, 10mm, platinum
and diamonds, 17
jewel manual wind,
1930s. *$995*
*Watch courtesy of Derek
Dier, WatchesToBuy.com*

ROYCE
• Lady's, platinum and
diamond, 15 jewel manual
wind, 16mm. *$1,900*
*Watch courtesy of Derek
Dier, WatchesToBuy.com*

SAVOY
- Military, 30mm, chromium case, 15 jewel manual wind. *$650*

Watch courtesy of Derek Dier, WatchesToBuy.com

SICURA
- Insta-light, 17 jewel manual wind, 39mm, circa 1970. *$550*

Watch courtesy of Derek Dier, WatchesToBuy.com

SWISS
- Chronograph, circa 1950s, 18K pink gold, three piece with inner metal dust cap, rectangular pushers, *$1,300*

Watch courtesy of Heritage Auction Galleries

SWISS
- Lady's, enamel inset, 16.5mm, chromium case, 15 jewel manual wind. *$450*

Watch courtesy of Derek Dier, WatchesToBuy.com

VIP
- "Memosail" yachting 10-minute timer in stainless steel, circa 1975. *$725*

Watch courtesy of Tim and Reyne Haines

WEBER
- 22mm, gold filled, 17 jewel manual wind, circa 1950s. *$200*

Watch courtesy of Derek Dier, WatchesToBuy.com

WATCH TERMINOLOGY

Alarm: An option on the watch that allows you to be notified at a pre-set time.

Analog: A watch that illustrates the time by pointing to the numbers or markers on the dial.

Automatic Wind: A watch that is mechanical, yet winds by the movement from the wearer instead of being wound at the stem.

Battery Reserve Indicator: A feature designed to indicate a soon-to-be-dead battery. The second hand will move at 2-second increments instead of 1.

Bezel: The ring surrounding the dial of the watch.

Bracelet: The band of the watch. The bracelet is sometimes changeable, sometimes integrated.

Bubble Back: A term coined by Rolex to describe a model of watch produced from the 1930s to the 1950s. This model of watch had a "bubble like" back, and was waterproof.

Cabochon: An uncut stone often mounted on the tip of the watch's crown.

Calendar: A feature on a watch offering the date of the month, and sometimes the day/date.

Center Second: A feature found in the center of the dial; smaller hand that marks the seconds.

Chapter Ring: A ring on the dial of the watch that illustrates the numbers or symbols of the hours.

Chronograph: A timepiece with the ability to record elapsed time, in minutes or seconds.

Chronometer: A watch offering the highest of accuracy. A chronometer is designed to ensure exact measurement of time.

Complicated Movement: Features on a watch that go beyond telling time, such as calendar, moon phase, chronograph, alarms, etc.

Cosmograph: A chronograph, originally designed by Rolex, that offers the tachymeter scale on the bezel, instead of on the dial.

Crown: The part attached to the stem used to wind the watch, and also set the date and time.

Crystal: The glass, plastic, or sapphire cover on the watch dial.

Depth Alarm: This feature is used on diving watches to alert when a pre-set depth is reached.

Dial: The face of a watch.

Electronic Watch (quartz): A watch that is battery-powered instead of manual or automatic wind.

Integrated Bracelet: A watch band that does not detach from the head of the watch.

Jewels: Synthetic sapphires, rubies, or diamonds are often used within watch movements to create less friction (metal on metal) or wear. The more jewels, the higher the quality of movement.

Jump Hour: A separate indicator set into the dial of a watch that moves exactly every hour on the hour.

Kinetic: A watch that runs on magnetic charge instead of a battery. The watch stays wound by the movement of the wearer's arm, creating a magnetic charge that is turned into electricity. Seiko was the creator of the kinetic watch.

Lap Timer: A feature that allows the wearer to time segments of a race. Once the segment has ended, the timer is stopped and resets back to zero. These are favorites of runners.

LCD (liquid crystal display): A digital watch display, made up of numerous pixels arrayed in front of a light source or reflector that illuminates the time.

Lugs: The "arms" of the watch to which the watch band attaches.

Luminescence: A thin layer of zinc sulfide painted on the hands of earlier watches so that they would glow in the dark. It was banned in the 1950s.

Mechanical Movement: The inner workings of a watch that runs on a mainspring and balance wheel. These movements are not battery operated.

Minute Repeater: An additional feature on a watch that chimes on the hour, quarter hour and minute.

Moon Phase: A lunar calendar on a watch that continuously changes, showing the different phases of the moon.

Power Reserve Indicator: An indicator on a watch showing how much power is left before the watch needs to be wound again.

Pusher: A button on the side of a watchcase most often used for a stopwatch function.

Quartz Movement: A watch that is powered by a quartz crystal. Quartz movements tend to be more accurate than mechanical movements.

Rose (Pink) Gold: A lower-karat gold that is pink in color.

Rotating Bezel: The ring on the outside of the watch that can be turned. This feature is popular with divers, as it allows them to track the exact immersion time.

Sapphire Crystal: A high-caliber crystal for a watch dial that is scratch resistant.

Screw-Down Crown: A crown on a watch that screws down tight to make it water resistant. This feature was originally created by Rolex.

Shock Resistant: A watch that can withstand the impact of being dropped.

Skeleton Watch: A watch usually without a dial, which allows you to see the inner workings of the movement. These movements are often heavily engraved.

Stopwatch: A watch that can measures time in short intervals.

Sub-Dial: A smaller dial set within the main dial that can be used to track seconds, or to illustrate the date.

Sub-Second: A smaller dial, usually at the 6 o'clock mark, that tracks seconds.

Tachymeter: A device on a watch that measures the speed traveled to a specific distance.

Water Resistant: A watch that has been sealed to help protect against water damage. This does not indicate the watch is waterproof. Note: Some watches will state the water depth it has been tested for.

Winding Stem: The crown on the side of the watch that winds the mainspring.

World Time Dial: An additional dial on the outer edge of the main dial that tells the time around the world.

RESOURCES

CLUBS AND ASSOCIATIONS CONTACTS

New and seasoned collectors, alike, love sharing their collecting enthusiasm. There are many clubs and organizations to expand your knowledge, and allow you to meet others with similar collecting interests.

THE NATIONAL ASSOCIATION OF WATCH AND CLOCK COLLECTORS

Founded in 1943, the National Association of Watch and Clock Collectors Inc. is a nonprofit scientific organization that serves as a unique educational, cultural and social resource for its membership and the public at large. It is headquartered in Columbia, Pa. Members include hobbyists, students, educators, casual collectors and professionals in retail and manufacturing trades. The one common bond is a fascination with the art and science of timekeeping. There are more than 175 chapters worldwide. *(www.nawcc.org)*

THE AMERICAN WATCHMAKERS-CLOCKMAKERS INSTITUTE

AWCI is the premier professional international organization dedicated to preserving and promoting the highest standards of workmanship in the horological crafts. It is the role of AWCI to set the standard of excellence applied to the quality of instruction for both the repair and restoration practices that are taught worldwide to watch and clockmakers.

AWCI was organized in 1960 as the American Watchmakers Institute (AWI) as this nation's first unified horological organization. It combined the members of the United Horological Association of America (UHAA) with those of the Horological Institute of America (HIA). There are 21 chapters in the United States. *(www.awi-net.org)*

• • • • • • • • • • • • •

INTERNET SITES

HAUTE HORLOGERIE:

An educational Web site for some of the leading watch brands in the world. It includes museum exhibition information, preservation, etc., with a timeline from the 13th century to the present. *(www.hautehorlogerie.com)*

ONLINE GROUPS

About Time: The Pocket Watch, Wrist Watch and Timepiece Discussion Group. About Time is a friendly and intelligent forum for collectors, dealers, hobbyists and professionals interested in sharing information on horology, vintage and new pocket and wristwatches, other timepieces, and timepiece repair and restoration. http://groups.yahoo.com/group/About_Time/

WATCHNETWORK: (HTTP://WWW.WATCHNETWORK.COM)
The WatchNetwork brings together some of the most respected people in the watch industry. Using their extensive knowledge, they are committed to creating the most informative watch site on the internet.

CLASSIC WATCH: (HTTP://WWW.CLASSICWATCH.COM/DISCUS/INDEX.HTML)
A longstanding Web site offering numerous discussion boards for the watch enthusiast. Covering Swiss, military and American timepieces with a strong emphasis on Jaeger-LeCoultre

WATCHGEEKS: (HTTP://WWW.WATCHGEEKS.NET)
Discussion board for watch enthusiasts. Most watch discussions are related to contemporary watches.

• • • • • • • • • • • • •

FOR MORE INFORMATION, CONTACT THESE CONTRIBUTORS:

ANTIQUORUM
www.antiquorum.com
595 Madison Ave.
New York, NY 10022
212-750-1103

BONHAMS &
BUTTERFIELDS
www.bonhams.com
7601 W. Sunset Blvd.
Los Angeles, CA 90046-2714
323-850-7500

CLEVES & LONNEMAN
JEWELERS
Charlie Cleves
319 Fairfield Ave.
Bellevue, KY 41073
859-261-3636

DEREK DIETER
www.watchestobuy.com
sales@watchestobuy.com
519-808-7355

HERITAGE AUCTION
GALLERIES
www.HA.com
3500 Maple Ave., 17th Floor
Dallas, TX 75219
800-872-6467

LESLIE HINDMAN
AUCTIONEERS
www.lesliehindman.com
1338 West Lake St.
Chicago, IL 60607
312-280-1212

SKINNER INC.
www.skinnerinc.com
63 Park Plaza
Boston, MA 02116
617-350-5400

ABOUT THE AUTHOR

Appraiser and media personality Reyne Haines, who specializes in 20th-century decorative arts, is regularly called upon to appraise collectibles ranging from antique watches to $20 million paintings. Her appraising skills are in demand by investment firms, estates and charity auctions.

Reyne frequently appears as an expert in the media, including as a recurring special guest on The Early Show on CBS and in numerous publications including The Wall Street Journal, The Washington Post, The Chicago Tribune, The Los Angeles Times, Home & Garden, Hemisphere Magazine, Worth Magazine, TV Guide, Family Circle Magazine, Time Out New York, Traditional Home, Romantic Home, Inspire Magazine and Collectors Weekly. She is also a blogger for The Huffington Post and may be heard on Martha Stewart Living Radio on the Sirius Satellite Radio Network.

In 2003, Reyne wrote The Art of Glass for the Dayton, Ohio, Art Institute. She has contributed to books including Antiques Roadshow Collectibles by Carol Prisant and Adventures at the Auction by Leslie Hindman. Reyne penned the introduction to the 2009 Warman's Companion — Watches and a chapter on investing in Tiffany for the 2010 edition of Warman's Antiques and Collectibles Price Guide.

Reyne's professional background has included working as a model, news announcer and journalist. She continuously expands her expertise into new areas; developing original television programming, authoring trade books and using broadcast media and the Internet to connect with an avid, national fan base of collectors. Reyne is the owner of The Finer Things in New York City, a company that acquires and sells luxury goods for clients at auction and privately. She works and lives in New York City and in Houston.

Contact: reyne@reyne.com

INDEX

A

Aaron Lufkin Dennison, 119
Abercrombie & Fitch, 146
Abraham Lincoln, 115, 213
Acapulco 666, 51
Accutron, 34-36
Ace, 118
Achille Ditesheim, 144
Admiral's Cup, 52
Advisor, 219, 222
Aegler, 188
Airflight, 68
Air-King, 193, 197
Alain Perrin, 42
Albert Wittnauer, 237
Alberto Santos-Dumont, 42
Alfred Van Cleef, 234
Alpina, 78
American Horology Company, 235
American Watchmakers Institute,
  250
André Heiniger, 189
Andy Warhol, 8, 144
Antoine LeCoultre, 122
Antoine Norbert de Patek, 175
Apollo XI, 166
Appleton Tracey & Co., 235
Aqua Lung, 25
Aquadura Crown, 143
Atlantic, 118, 134
Austria, 31
Autavia, 114
AWCI, 250

B

Baignoire, 42
Barcelona, 212
Baron, 82
Basel, 14, 67
Belforte, 23
Beluga, 59
Benjamin Lazrus, 23
Berlin, 31
Biel, 143
Bienne, 50, 67, 149
Blackstone, 118
Blue Hawaii, 94
Boston Watch Co., 235
Brandt & Son, 149

British Army, 64
British Royal Air Force, 149, 189
Bugatti, 58
Bullhead Chronograph, 37
Bund, 113

C

Calatrava, 178
Calendomatic, 144
Carl Edouard, 31
Casebook, 188
Celebrity, 10-11
Cellini, 207-208
Celtic, 149
Centiure, 44
Certina, 241
César Brandt, 149
Charles Arpels, 234
Charles-Emile Tissot, 216
Chronomat, 28, 30
Chronometer, 9, 31, 63, 188, 191,
  205-207, 223, 238, 248
Chronostop, 157
Chrono-Timer, 71
Cincinnati, 68
Coach, 144
Collectors Club, 9
Columbus, 68
Comet, 136
Compax, 225
Compur, 225
Constantin de Gorski, 20
Constellation, 155-156, 160, 170-
  171, 173
Contantin Girard, 65
Corvette, 201
Cosmic, 169
Cosmograph, 188-189, 248
Cosmonaute, 28
Countess Koscowicz, 8
Crazy Hours, 241
Cricket, 234
Curvex, 68, 74-75, 80-92

D

D. Gruen & Son, 68
Datejust, 191, 194-195, 208
Datometer, 143
Davis Cup, 216

Dietrich Gruen, 68
Dodson, 103
Duotone, 69

E

Ebauches SA, 219
Edmond Jaeger, 42, 122
Edouard Bovet, 27
Edouard Heuer, 113
Eduard Jakob Gübelin, 93
Edward-Auguste Piguet, 14
Edwige Girod, 32
El Primero, 238
Electro Chron, 237
Elvis Presley, 94
Emperador, 186
Empress Eugenie, 42
Enicar, 241
Ernest Borel, 26
Ernest Francillon, 134
Ernest Schneider, 28
Ernst, 31
Eska, 241
Eterna-Matic, 63
Everest, 94, 99
Explorer I, 200

F

Fellows and Schel, 235
Ferrari, 65
Fifty Fathoms, 25
Flieger, 113
Flightmaster, 168
Florentine Ariosto Jones, 119
Formula One, 113
France, 26, 43, 46, 229
Franchi Minotti, 5
Franck Muller, 241
Francois Czapek, 175
Fred Gruen, 68
Frederic William Dubois, 223
French Navy, 219
Frey, 242

G

Gay Frères, 182
Gen. Juan Peron, 225
Genex, 10
George Favre-Jacot, 238

George G. Schaeren, 143
Georges Piaget, 184
Georges-Auguste Leschot, 229
Glashutte, 13
GMT, 30, 199
Golden Bridge, 52-53
Golden Shadow, 225
Golf, 47, 54, 62, 219
Grenchen, 56, 63
Gucci, 26
Gurzelen, 149

H
Half Hunter, 25
Hans Wilsdorf, 188, 219
Harry Truman, 225
Haute Horlogerie, 250
Hawthorne, 117
Helbein Brothers, 112
Helios, 242
Helvetia, 149-150
Henri Rieckel, 149
Heraldic Emblem, 219
Hong Kong, 225
Horological Institute of America, 250
Horologist, 237
Horology, 188, 223, 235, 251
Hoverta, 242
Hunter, 25, 83
Hurricane, 202

I
Il Destriero Scafusia, 119
Ingenieur, 119
Ingersoll, 242

J
J. Eugene Robert, 237
Jaccard, 242
Jacques Cousteau, 25
Jacques Didisheim, 133
Jacques-David LeCoultre, 122
Jean Cocteau, 225
Jean-Adrien Philippe, 175
Jean-Francois Bautte, 65
Jean-Frederic Bovet, 27
Jean-Marc Vacheron, 229
Jehan-Jacques Blancpain, 25
Jo Siffert, 114
John Harwood, 9
Josef Gerard, 63
Jules-Louis Audemars, 14

Jura, 149
Jürgen Jürgensen, 133

K
Kallista, 229
Kew Observatory, 188
Kinetic, 249
Kingmatic, 146
Kintaro Hattori, 212
Kon-Tiki, 63

L
La Chaux-de-Fonds, 52, 57, 59, 64,
   133, 144, 234
Lacoste, 144
Lady Tiger, 61
Landeron, 49, 235, 237
Lap Timer, 249
Larpent & Jürgensen, 133
LCD, 166, 212, 249
Le Brassus, 14
Le Jour, 243
Le Locle, 58, 223, 234, 239
Le Must, 42
LeCoultre & Cie, 122
Lemania, 235
Leon Breitling, 28
Leonard-Frederic Nardin, 223
Longines, 134-142
Lexon, 243
Liberty Eagle, 52, 55
Lindbergh, 34, 134
Linwood, 104
Lord Elco, 243
Lord Elgin, 61-62
Lordmatic, 212
Louis-Francois Cartier, 42
Louis-Ulysse Chopard, 48
Lucerne, 31, 93
Lucien Piccard, 243-244

M
Majesty, 86
Marconi, 10
Marie Perregaux, 65
Marine Chronometer, 188, 223
Mark XI, 119
Masonic, 177, 217, 236
Master Mariner, 127
Masterpiece Line, 102
Mauboussin, 132
Maurice Ditisheim Fabrique Vulcain, 234

Medana, 244
Memosail, 247
Memovox, 93, 122, 125-127
Meritus, 192
Miley Cyrus, 56
Military, 13, 37, 60, 62, 73, 94, 146,
   164, 205, 245, 247, 251
Millionometer, 122
Mimo, 244
Monaco, 114
Montbrillant Eclipse, 29
Mort Clayman, 133
Moscow, 26
Movado, 42, 144-148, 214, 225
Mt. Everest, 94
Multifort, 143
Museum, 63-64, 144, 149, 250
Mystérieuse, 137-138
Mystery Dial, 68-69, 232

N
Nagano, 212
NASA, 149
National Association of Watch and
   Clock Collectors, 11, 250
National Watch, 61
Nautilus, 176, 181
Navitimer, 4, 28-29
Navy Seals, 219
Neil Armstrong, 149
New Yorker, 115
Nivada, 56, 245
Nivada Grenchen, 56
Normandie, 245
Numa-Emile Descombes, 224

O
Odyssey, 96
Olma, 245
Onyx, 184
Orator, 245
Orchid, 211
Oyster, 188-198, 200-206, 208, 210,
   219-222

P
Pacer, 100
Padellone, 205
Panthere, 42, 47
Pantographic Tool, 229
Paris Exhibition, 175
Pasha, 42, 47

Patria, 149
Paul Breguette, 54, 59
Paul Mercier, 20
Perry, 102
Pilot, 28, 42, 113, 119
Pink Banana, 179
Piping Rock, 94
Piquette, 245
Plan-les-Ouates, 229
Polaris, 96, 98, 124
Porsche, 119
Premier, 30, 250
President, 115, 196
Prince, 207, 220, 222
Pulsemeter, 71

Q
Queen Victoria, 175
Quincy Jones, 56

R
Radio Signal, 28
Rado, 246
Railroad, 34, 36, 94-95, 115
Ranchero, 163
Rattrapante System, 60
Reflet, 26
Rene Bannwart, 52
Reverso, 122, 131
Richemont Group, 229
Richeville, 65
Roadster, 44
Robert Peron, 20
Rolco, 10
Rolls Royce, 52
Romulus, 52
Roy C. King, 32
Royal Oak, 14, 17, 19
Royalite, 201
Royce, 52, 246

S
Saint Christopher, 149
Samuel Curtis, 235
Santos, 42, 46
Sapporo, 212
Saratoga, 51
Saturno, 203
Savitar, 100
Savoy, 247
Scandinavia, 48

Schaffhausen, 119-121
Scott Carpenter, 28
Sea-Dweller Submariner, 198
Seamaster, 151, 158-167
Seashark, 244
Sea Wolf, 239-240
Shipmate, 146
Sicura, 247
Simone Ries, 52
Singing Bird, 32
Sky Chief, 24
Skyrocket, 201
Solvil, 57
Sovereign, 23
Speedking, 193, 205
Speedmaster, 2, 149, 166-167
Speedsonic Lobster, 169
Speedy 125, 167
Springfield, 115
St. Imier, 28, 113, 134
Staybrite, 168-169
Stelux Holding Group, 225
Steve McQueen, 200
Stuart, 115
Submariner, 11, 198, 200, 219, 222
Super Ocean, 29
Swatch Group, 143
Swiss National Exhibition, 59, 229

T
Tachymeter, 248-249
Tank, 42-43, 45-47, 184
Taylor Swift, 56
Tazio Nuvolari, 60
Telemetre Dial, 30
Thor Heyerdahl, 63
TIAS, 6
Tiger Woods, 219
Titus, 57
Tommy Hilfiger, 144
Top Hat, 179
Top-Time, 29
Tortue, 42
Tourbillion, 9, 25, 225
Triumph, 87, 90
Tropical Dial, 168
Tudor Rose, 219
Tudor Submariner, 219, 222
Tuning Unisonic, 225
Turner, 102
TWA, 94

U
Unicorn, 10
United Airlines, 94
Unitime, 30
Universal Demonstration, 144
Universal Exposition, 14
Universal Watch, 224
Urs Schild, 63

V
Valjoux, 30, 112-114, 235, 237, 239, 241-243
Van Horn, 97
Ventura, 94, 101
Veri-Thin, 68, 70, 72, 74-77, 85-86, 90
Viceroy, 206
Victor II, 101
Visodate, 218
Vital Bueche, 32

W
W.J. Savage, 68
Waltham Improvement Co., 235
Warren Boston, 235
Watford, 32
Watson, 102
Weber, 247
Weems, 136
Westfield, 38
White House, 213
William Baume, 20
William II, 31
Wilsdorf & Davis, 188
World Series, 94
World Time, 36, 249

Y
Yacht Timer, 113
Yankee Watch, 94
Yankees, 94

Z
Zenith Radio Corp, 238
Zephyr, 196
Zodiac, 239-240

MORE TIME SAVVY GUIDES

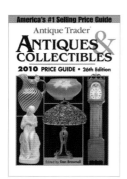

ANTIQUE TRADER ANTIQUES & COLLECTIBLES 2010 PRICE GUIDE
26th Edition
Edited by Dan Brownell

Inside this, America's top-selling collectibles price guide you'll find 7,500 listings, current pricing, and 4,000 color photos, to help you identify and assess the value of everything from pottery and glass to furniture, fine art, toys and timepieces. Plus, you'll find new market trend reports and 20 Trader Tips – including key insight about a segment of the hobby and the items within it.

Softcover • 6 x 9 • 816 pages
4,000 color photos
Item# Z4968 • **$19.99**

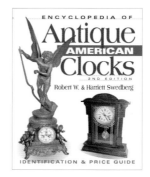

ENCYCLOPEDIA OF ANTIQUE AMERICAN CLOCKS
2nd Edition
by Robert W. & Harriet Swedberg

This all-inclusive guide features furniture-size timepieces, including shelf, novelty, grandfather and wall clocks, among others. Each listings includes a color photo, pricing and a hearty description to help with identifying the clocks in your collection with ease.

Softcover • 8¼ x 10⅞ • 368 pages
900+ color photos
Item# WCLK2 • **$29.99**

WATCHES
by Dean Judy

This timepiece tell-all features 1,000+ color photos of the most elegant to the most economical watches. Each listing includes details to help with identifying each watch, and current market pricing to aid in determining the value. Whether you're a fan of Elgin, Omega, Timex or a host of other makers, this beautifully arranged and informative guide is good investment.

Softcover • 5 x 8 • 272 pages
1,000+ color photos
Item# Z1922 • **$17.99**

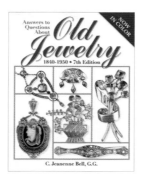

ANSWERS TO QUESTIONS ABOUT OLD JEWELRY
7th Edition
by C. Jeanenne Bell G.G.

This comprehensive and full-color guide to all things jewelry also includes select watches, displayed in beautiful photographs with accompanied by key identifying details. Whether you also enjoy additional types of jewelry, this guide is a valuable reference to have in your library.

Softcover • 8¼ x 10⅞ • 448 pages
2,000 color photos
Item#Z2343 • **$29.99**

WARMAN'S CIVIL WAR COLLECTIBLES CD
by John F. Graf

An indispensable and beautifully illustrated guide to Civil War memorabilia, among the items and artifacts included in this easy-to-search CD are personal mementos including watches and timepieces. With so many intriguing artifacts from the war, this CD serves as a valuable resource.

Format: CD
Item# Z4970 • **$24.99**

SHOP.COLLECT.COM ~ FOR EVERYTHING YOU COLLECT